SALLY JAMES'

Almost legendary

POP INTERVIEWS

EEL PIE PUBLISHING

ACKNOWLEDGEMENTS

My thanks extend to so many people who helped me get this book together:

Judy Totton, Simon Porter, Chris Griffin, Mike Perry, Clive Banks, Peter Price, John Smith, Kim Glover, Lisa Sayers and Hilary Walker for getting the folk together.

To Linda Simpson, Susanne Tovey, Sue Cheah and my mum for spending hours slaving over a hot typewriter.

To all the photographers (especially my dad) for clicking their buttons at the right time.

And my husband Mike, for putting up with me through it all!

PHOTO CREDITS

Adam Ant	*W. Gullachsen/A.T.V.*
Bad Manners	*Bert Cann*
Kate Bush	*Bert Cann*
Phil Collins	*Bert Cann*
Roger Daltrey	*W. Gullachsen/A.T.V.*
Sheena Easton	*W. Gullachsen/A.T.V.*
Dave Edmunds	*Bert Cann*
Motorhead	*Simon Porter*
Rick Parfitt	*W. Gullachsen/A.T.V.*
Spandau Ballet	*George Bodnar*
Toyah	*W. Gullachsen/A.T.V.*
Ultravox	*Simon Fowler*
Kim Wilde	*Bert Cann*

First published in 1981 by Eel Pie Publishing Ltd, 45 Broadwick Street, London W1V 1FS.

ISBN 0 906008 28 X

Printed and bound in Great Britain by R. J. Acford, Industrial Estate, Chichester, Sussex.

INTRODUCTION

For the past eight years I have been involved in presenting Saturday morning programmes – first 'Saturday Scene' for London Weekend Television, and for the last four years, ATV's 'Tiswas'. During that time I have interviewed just about anybody who is anybody in the pop world. When it came to getting this book together it was very difficult for me to decide who should be in it. I hope you'll agree that I've chosen a good cross-section and that you'll enjoy reading it as much as I've enjoyed getting it together. I've spent many hours compiling these interviews and travelled all over the place to do them – from the splendour of Roger Daltrey's farm to the cramped conditions of my ATV dressing room for Rick Parfitt, finishing off at the N.E.C. before a Quo concert with over 10,000 fans chanting outside! I interviewed in record company offices for Spandau Ballet, recording studios for Toyah and even had a roof-top chat high above the city of London with Motorhead!

The world of pop is exciting and fast moving. I hope through this book you'll get to know some of its top personalities as well as I do.

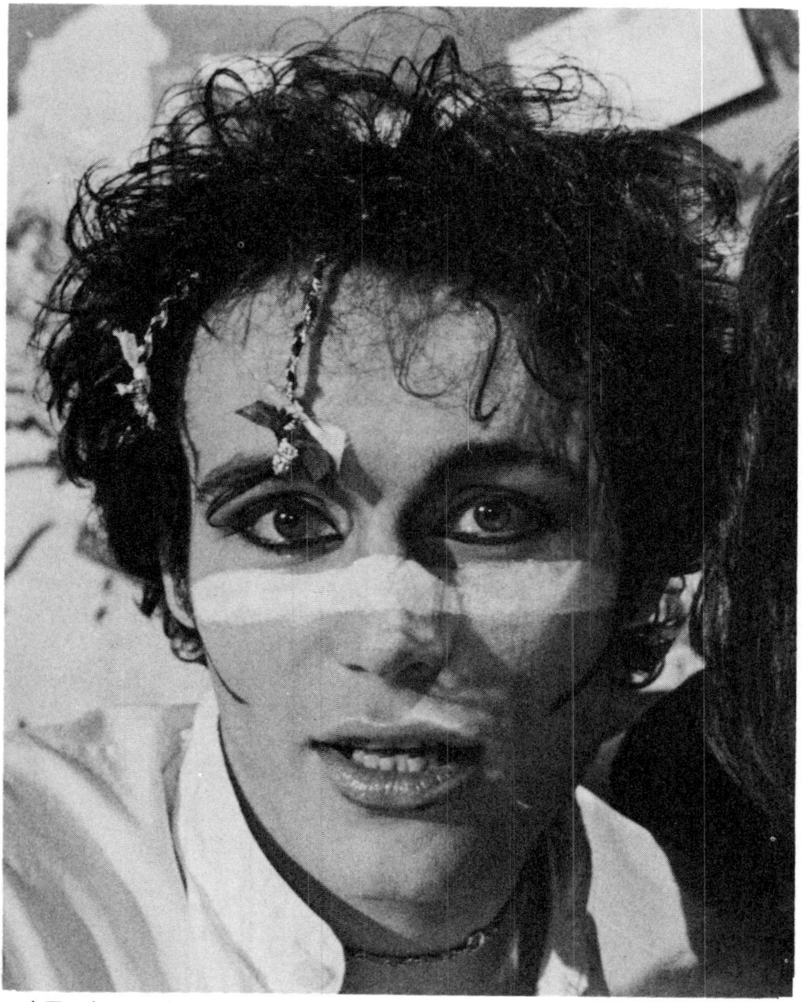

ADAM ANT

Adam was unfortunately out of the country the whole time I was preparing this book, so I couldn't meet up with him for a chat. We had met, of course, when he appeared on 'Tiswas'; however, I did manage to track him down by phone in Fowey, Cornwall and over a crackling G.P.O. line we had a chat . . .

Sally: You've been touring all over Europe – doing about fifty gigs in all. How have all those different countries reacted to you?

Adam: In some places it's been newer and more of a surprise and maybe too much for some people, but I think the reaction has been very good. All the gigs have been sold out; they've all been quite exciting for us anyway and the audiences seem to go away quite happy.

Sally: Where has it all been a surprise for them?

Adam: In some places where they know the band slightly through TV shows, they're not quite tuned in to it. The idea hasn't been channelled through and when the band turn up live, I think it's all a bit too much; it can be a bit overwhelming. In a way that's good because it keeps your feet on the ground and you remember there's still a lot of people that don't know anything about you so you've got to work even harder. In all the English speaking places, like the Channel Islands, the kids turned up in all sorts of outfits which were really colourful. It also happened in a few places in Europe.

Sally: What about America? What was that like?

Adam: They were very receptive and really made us welcome. We were very surprised at the reaction at such an early stage in America. I was very warmed towards the American people; the kids were great – they came along dressed up. In L.A. they even built pirate ships.

Sally: What's the record situation for you over there?

Adam: The album's in the top fifty. It's sold about three quarters of a million. If anything, it has laid a foundation for follow-up work.

Sally: Did you have to play any difficult venues?

Adam: I think we had to do two gigs on this tour in Europe that we wouldn't normally play. You can't apply the same sort of gig situation in Europe that you can in England. On the tours we have to play large and small. We've had problems getting the gear in, problems with lighting and various things, but you hope the kids like the show, then you can go back to much better venues next time.

Sally: In a way, aren't you going back a couple of steps in the other countries?

Adam: Yes, but that doesn't matter. It's early days yet. I think it's good because you have to work that bit harder as you don't know what's coming each night. You know one night you could be on the stage and you can dance quite freely, then the next night you dance three paces back and you're in the middle of the drum kit. So you learn to have a lot more faith in the show and the music than what's going on. I think you rely far more on atmosphere than situations.

Sally: Very exciting, I should think. I gather one of the tribes in America was upset with your make-up?

Adam: Yes. When I went over at Christmas the North American Indian Community Centre in New York had seen my album cover. They thought it was extending the stereotype of the American Indian that they're trying to get rid of; they felt it was a bit of a rip-off in a bang bang Cowboy and Indians way, which upset me.

As soon as I arrived in America, I went straight to their headquarters in New York and said, 'Look, it isn't like this, it's really something spiritual to me, something I've researched. If you think that I'm perpetuating any bad stereotype of the North American Indian nation, come to my show and if you think that I'm exploiting your culture then I'll gladly take the line off and take the feathers off.' Ten of them came to the show, and they loved it. They wrote an official letter to C.B.S. saying they found no part of the show offensive. In fact, they found it very exciting. One of the music papers blew it up because they don't like the band. In fact the Centre wrote a letter to the journalist who said that, saying, 'You have no right to say that about Adam and the Ants because we find nothing offensive about it'. I think we'll be doing a concert in the States for them.

Sally: Let's go back a bit. How old were you when you first became interested in music?

Adam: I started late. I always liked music but I didn't pick up an instrument or start playing until I was about thirteen or fourteen, and then it was just playing about. I started to learn but didn't continue it, but when I was about fourteen or fifteen I stuck in there and learned the guitar. Then I learned bass guitar and I was in a few small groups, then I just took over singing.

Sally: After that you went to art school. How important was music to you then?

Adam: At school, music was a secondary part of my life, but the more I worked at art the more I realised the sort of ideas I was trying to express visually were much better expressed through music. The conflict between the two became quite strong. In the end I had to be honest with myself and I chose music.

I started, more or less, to work on the idea of a group about a year before I left college. I was thinking about this group a long, long time before I actually got on the stage, and I'd written all the songs by the time the other members of the group joined.

Sally: How did record companies react to your having the whole plan worked out?

Adam: When I was with Decca I did the drawings for 'Young Parisiennes' under a pseudonym, but there was quite a bit of trouble. Certain people at the record company had faith in it. I think at the time they realised that it was a little bit unusual to have somebody who was interested in all parts of the machinery that go into making a record. At Decca for instance, Mike Smith was one of the people that stuck out for me after that situation; but it was very difficult to get the people above to go along with it. So I left there and I went to an independent company because I really wanted to put it together and there I could. I worked on the logo and the style for Adam and the Ants, and modified that, so by the time I negotiated with a major company I really had ideas that I felt were relevant to the sort of product I was putting out. I don't think the word is control because I like to delegate; but there's got to be clarity and there's got to be one decision.

Sally: You've changed your look quite a lot, haven't you?

Adam: There are certain things in this look that I've retained.

I've retained a piece of everything, so I look at it as a kind of progression in what I wear. There's absolutely no way that I could have arrived at something as bizarre as the look at the moment without having gone through every single phase of Adam and the Ants. I'd gone through a period wearing kilts and tartan, then the Samurai, the warrior thing, and then we sat down and we did songs and there was a sudden clarity of topic – a warrior pride – very heroic. All the things I wear are basically heroic. The bows are from Blackbeard who was the most famous of all pirates. The tribal side of things has always fascinated me, as has Japanese Kabouki make-up and all sorts of other make-up. Even the multi-coloured faces in 'Apocalypse Now' show ways of using your face to present an idea.

Sally: Do you still take a diary and notebook everywhere with you?

Adam: Yes. I just put down lyrics and drawings and ideas. I've got about twenty of them. They were really helpful in my recent problems with Decca when they wanted to release my old demos, because I could actually prove that I'd written the songs at a certain time and prove that they were demos by the fact that they were recorded in that way. It's no different to what a painter does. A painter always has a little book with him. I'm lost without a pen and a little book.

Sally: When do you have time to write the next album? Do you do it while you're on the road?

Adam: All the time. It's a constant thing. Marco and I wrote the next album that we're about to record about six months ago. We'd written a couple of songs by the time we'd finished the 'Kings' album. We went in the studio and demo'd the songs to see how they sounded. We don't tend to look in terms of doing one album and writing so many songs for it. We write a whole lot of songs and then we find that some are up to it and some aren't.

Sally: If you wrote most of the album six months ago have you not found that you've come up with better things than you originally intended for the album?

Adam: No, not really. We're very methodical, Marco and me. We write at a very slow pace. The fact that we wrote nine songs six months ago was because we'd been writing for nine months before that. We've become more and more methodical and much more careful about what we write. We just go into a studio, the two of us, and we put down all the instruments ourselves in a rough format and basically there's very little difference, apart from the production, between that and the final thing. If I played you the demo of 'Stand and Deliver' you'd think it was a rough version of the actual finished single, but it was made in a sixteen-track studio with Marco and me banging things together.

Sally: Do you always write with Marco?

Adam: We take it as a very classical writing partnership, whatever we do. It's kind of fifty-fifty and we prefer it that way.

Sally: It seems that since you teamed up with him you've started writing more commercial things, or is that just coincidence?

Adam: I just think that he had a lot of influence, a lot of ideas that worked well with mine and we both like to keep things very simple. We're totally opposite people, apart from when we work. We know what we don't want to hear on a record, so we put down what we do want to hear.

Sally: What about your relationship with the rest of the band? There's been much written of how you make all the decisions and tell them what to do, that they're very much your backing band.

Adam: I don't look at it that way. I've had several line-ups. I've been in groups where everybody's writing and I can't work under those conditions. I either write alone or with Marco – we don't fish it out. We don't want a situation where it branches out too much; it causes arguments. Everybody in the group has the same kind of commitment and everybody's treated identically, only there's far more pressure on myself and Marco outside of performing, which is fine. I don't look at the band as session men. This band works really hard on stage; everybody's got a different personality, everybody's acknowledged for being themselves.

Sally: Do you demand a lot from them?

Adam: No more than I demand from myself. If I can do it I expect them to be able to do it. That doesn't really arise because they are all very professional people. It's just a matter of whether people respect you enough to be led by you. If you look at a group like Roxy Music, Bryan Ferry's quite certainly the leader of that group – that's how the group works.

When I was a kid, I bought Roxy Music records and I loved that look, but by the time I actually got to see Roxy Music they'd changed and I never forgot it. I think that if kids want to see the look, then they should be able to see it live and in all its glory. It may take me a year to do the whole world, it may take me two years, but when everybody's seen it – and I've only got Australia and Japan to do now – then I may do other things. By the end of a year I think you are, in fact, weary of putting on the same face every night.

I've already designed the way I want to look next and I've been thinking about it for the last six months, but quite honestly I welcome the chance to tour for six months because I have a desire to play it live to the kids. I like the idea of kids not having the same frustration as I had.

Sally: So you've got the next thing worked out?

Adam: It was worked out three months ago. 'Stand and Deliver' was a bridge point, a slight modification, but the idea was there and the flavour of the video was there. I think things come along at their own pace and if you are constantly looking to change that means that you are a little bit insecure about what you want to do next.

Sally: So you will gradually change over the next few months?

Adam: It depends. I often think about whether things are actually new. Are people coming to see you, are they coming to see you dressed up, are they coming to see the kind of face you put on, are they coming to see you because they like your personality? I'd rather they liked me for what I am and what I sing, because I'm going to sing it a certain way that's me, that's my style. If I watch Elvis Presley I want to see the pelvis, the move, whatever he's wearing. I think Elvis was the great equaliser. One film he'd be a cowboy, then he'd be a G.I. He could be anything.

I sing certain songs with certain looks. When I sing songs like 'Car Trouble' I perform in a totally different way from the way I sing 'Dog Eat Dog' or 'Ant Music', because I've learnt more, so the next thing I do will be a development. I don't want it to chop and change. I think there are subtle ways of doing it by keeping the standard and quality of your music and your professionalism and presentation and using the best crews, best sound and best theatres. That's my biggest problem at the moment, getting the right theatre to play. If the place is unusual enough it makes the kids think, 'Why is he playing here?'

Sally: Do you have time for any private life at all, or does your whole life revolve around your work?

Adam: Well, I do. Most of my private life is just having a quiet meal or going out to the cinema or relaxing and taking it easy – going for walks. It's just very quiet, because I don't like clubs and I don't like going out to many places, but I just like a good meal and good company.

Sally: How much does a live performance take out of you?

Adam: Buckets of sweat. I go on with quite a lot of clothes on, quite a heavy set-up, but you build yourself up. You learn to be able to wear that amount of stuff over a period of time.

Sally: How long will you rest for now?

Adam: I don't know – probably a week, then I'll be bored and want to get back into it. I've got to get into the studio because we've to do one hell of an album. It's not going to be a sheep in wolf's clothing. It's going to be a wolf in wolf's clothing called 'Fighting'. I'm very, very excited by the next album. We've had much more time to work on it and I think it will be surprising.

BAD MANNERS

I first met Dougie alias Fatty, Buster Bloodvessel, or whatever you care to name him when his record company rang me up and said, 'Please will you let him spend a morning in your "Tiswas cage"?' Apparently, one of his unfulfilled ambitions was to be on the receiving end of buckets of water, slosh (a mixture of vegetable dye, shaving foam and water), soot and whatever else we cared to chuck at him.

'Our pleasure,' I replied. 'Send him up next Saturday.' I met up with him the day before and he was genuinely excited about the prospect of spending two hours locked up with a pile of loonies who should know better. Usually, half way through the programme, our people behind bars are not so enthusiastic about the cage as they originally thought they might be, but not Doug; he loved every minute and was actually screaming for more buckets! Well, there's no accounting for taste!

Sally: How long have you all been together now?

Doug: Bad Manners started six years ago at school. We didn't have any plans to do gigs or anything, we just sort of got together. We couldn't really play that well so we started rehearsing together. Then the chance came to play at the school but I had to sing with another band. After I did the gig, we confirmed that we were going to form Bad Manners. At the time it was Stoop Solo and the Sheep Starchers.

Sally: The whole concept was yours then, was it?

Doug: At the time, yes, but we all had the same sort of ideas. We wanted a band to have fun because we saw lots of boring bands about. We wanted to be a bit different so we got the ugliest people we could find – but we were all mates as well.

Sally: I gather there were about six of you then, but it got bigger than that . . .

Doug: Yes. We just started playing around and members left and new ones joined and we weren't quite sure who was in the band because we never wanted to be nasty to anyone by saying, 'You're not in the band', so it just grew and grew. There were sixteen of us once and we actually played a gig with all sixteen of us on stage.

Sally: It must have been ridiculous.

Doug: Yes. There were two bass players and I think there were five saxophonists.

Sally: So presumably you had to be a bit ruthless and get rid of a few people?

Doug: Sort of, yes. It got to a point where after that gig we sat down and said, "Who wants to be in the band?" Some people had other things to do and so it wasn't their prime concern to be in the band.

Sally: So it got down to nine of you.

Doug: Yes, it got down to eight, then nine. We weren't quite sure about the other sax player, because he went to America for a while but he'd been rehearsing while he was over there so he was really good when he came back.

Sally: What sort of gigs were you playing?

Doug: The smallest pub gigs that we could get, 'cause

nobody really wanted us, especially when they knew there were nine of us. We never used to split the money. We always put it into a kitty, so we'd say, 'That's the band's money and if we're lucky we might get some of it.'

Sally: Is there one person who decides what happens for the band or are all the decisions made jointly?

Doug: It's done very democratically. We have a big meeting and about the only time we argue is when we have to discuss business. We don't like doing that side of it but we have to. Usually we all come to an agreement; otherwise it's done on votes.

Sally: The nine of you write together, don't you? It sounds a nightmare trying to get nine people to collaborate on a song.

Doug: Well, when we start writing songs we sort of all go in and we sit down and say, 'Right, what are we going to do?' It's usually the guitarist or keyboard player who have something.

Sally: They have an idea for a song?

Doug: Yes, not a whole song. All they've got is maybe a few chords and they play them and we just jam along and then the brass go away into their own little section and we carry on without them and call them in when we're ready and then they come in and they work on the top. I have to be there at the beginning, then right through to the end because the lyrics don't get written till then.

Sally: Do all nine of you write the lyrics as well?

Doug: Sort of, yes. I've always got to be there because I'm the one who sings and we usually base it around me or something that's happened to me or ideas like that. When we were recording the first album we had a shortage of songs. We couldn't come up with any ideas and we were really getting worried, so we all went and got drunk on Special Brew and . . .

Sally: That was the idea.

Doug: Yes. We said, 'Let's write a song about it.' Good idea!

Sally: You said originally that the whole concept of Bad Manners was to have fun and that was it. Now you obviously have to take it more seriously, so are you still managing to make it for fun?

Doug: It was fun and it still is fun. All nine of us enjoy each other's company quite a lot so obviously wherever we go we brighten up the place, but it gets to a point where you think to yourself, 'Is this still fun?' We did a tour and we had about thirty dates one after the other. Half way through we were saying, 'Is this fun?' and we decided that we just had to take it as fun, but going on every night and forcing yourself to enjoy yourself . . .

Sally: It's not much fun, is it?

Doug: No, but it makes the band become more professional, because we weren't. We were a really untight band till we met our producer. He helped us a lot.

Sally: What about this following you seem to have with very young kids? I'm talking about under-tens. Did you ever think that would happen when you first started out?

Doug: We never really tried to appeal to just young kids. We've also got an over-forties following. There are lots of mums and dads really getting into us, which is fine.

Sally: You've had some problems with people who come to your gigs haven't you?

Doug: I think everyone seems to be getting that sort of trouble nowadays. It seems to be the in thing to fight at gigs but on the last British tour we had one spot of trouble out of about thirty dates. I think it was well exaggerated by the press; they seem to cash in on it which is terrible really. I don't think they know what harm they're doing.

Sally: Have you ever thought it might be nice to do some special gigs for children?

Doug: Yeah, we have. At the moment we are talking about a tour of disabled homes 'cause we are really into those kids. We played a gig once where lots of disabled kids came along and I auctioned my boiler suit for this little geezer; he was really small although he was a grown man of about twenty and I said, 'If I am going to do it you've got to come and auction it for me in front of a thousand people.' I didn't know whether I'd done the right thing, forcing him to do it but it turned out really great. Everybody cheered him as he came on, and when we came off he said that he was writing his life in a book and that this was one of his most memorable days. That really touched me.

Sally: You personally get all the publicity, don't you? How do the rest of the band feel about you being singled out?

Doug: They love to take the mickey out of me because of it. All the little kids come running up to us saying, 'Fatty, can I have your autograph'' and they don't do it to them and so they're constantly taking the mickey out of me for that. In fact, I think they would rather me have it than them.

Sally: This incredible tongue that you've got, didn't that start with yoga in front of the telly?

Doug: Yes. When I was about seven I used to bunk off school and every Monday morning there used to be this programme on telly, 'Yoga for health'. I used to watch it and I used to do the lion exercise where you stick your tongue out and look up to the ceiling. You are supposed to do it for about ten seconds, but I used to do it for about an hour or two and just leave it.

Sally: You were fascinated by it, were you?

Doug: Oh yes. Well, if you leave your tongue out for a while it dries up completely and it becomes another part of flesh on the outside – completely dry and it feels really weird. It doesn't feel like your tongue at all. I used to do this in front of the fire so it used to dry up really quick.

Sally: Do you see Bad Manners lasting for a long time?

Doug: I have got this really strong belief that Bad Manners can go on for a long time if we can get over all the little problems.

Sally: What little problems have you got then?

Doug: I dunno, you always get little problems like money and that sort of thing. Tiredness seems to be our biggest problem at the moment. We're all really exhausted.

Sally: That's the trouble when things start to happen, isn't it? Everybody wants you, you have no time off and you accept everything 'cause you must keep going and then it's very hard to switch off.

Doug: We could get work abroad for up to another two years on the bookings that we've been offered.

Sally: So exhaustion apart, you can see Bad Manners going on for quite some time.

Doug: Yes, I can because I know what the talent is inside Bad Manners.

Sally: And now you're on the third album, the one that's always the most criticised, the one that you're most judged on.

Doug: Yes. A lot of bands are pretty frightened to make their third album. We sort of stumbled into it and suddenly realised that we're making a third album, so we are not really taking it any different from the second. We're doing the Can-Can which is going to be very big, I can tell, with how it's going down with the kids. When we were in Ireland, we did three days where we played the Can-Can. Before that we had four days when we didn't. When we brought the Can-Can into the set it just made the whole show go ten times better.

Sally: What about your favourite single to date. Have you got one?

Doug: When Ne Ne Na Na Nu Nu was released it was really great for us because we've played that song in the set from day one. When we actually got it out and I heard it for the first time on the radio I felt really good inside, because we'd got a single out. So that's always something I remember, but I don't know what my favourite single is. 'Special Brew' has been the biggest, so it's easy to go for that one, but I think I would go for the one that's out at the moment, 'Just a Feeling'.

Sally: Do you get fed up with performing them over and over at gigs?

Doug: 'Lip up, Fatty' we're all very fed up with, we've done it so many times.

Sally: Why are you fed up with that one?

Doug: Probably because we've heard the Mike Sammes Singers or somebody like them doing it!

KATE BUSH

We met up at Joe Allen's restaurant in Covent Garden. Kate's not a person who usually eats lunch so she just had apple pie and cream before dashing off for a dance class. She goes about three times a week and one of those is a public dance class. You can just imagine Kate being put through her paces in front of other people but she says although she does get people staring at her, she thinks it's good for her – it brings her back to reality.

Sally: Kate, you're recording at the moment, aren't you?

Kate: What I am doing, rather than going in and deliberately thinking of doing an album, is just doing three tracks – two of which I definitely hope to be singles. So far we've finished one single and the B side, which is really great – a Donovan song. I've always wanted to do one of his songs because I've admired his music and his voice for years. I decided to do this song and through a coincidence it started happening. Someone asked me what I was doing for the B side while we were watching a Crystal Gayle show on TV. I was telling them I was going to do this Donovan song and all of a sudden Crystal Gayle said, '. . . and now my very special guest is Donovan' and you know we hadn't seen him on TV for years and years. It was really like it was right.

Sally: Fate.

Kate: Yes, and he came into the studio and did some backing vocals which is really great because I've always wanted to work with him.

Sally: When are you going to start on another album?

Kate: As soon as I can. What I thought was quite nice was working on two or three tracks at a time because then they do all get the right amount of love. If you've got ten songs you've got to spread out all this creative energy and try and make each one as good as the other, whereas if they're spaced out a bit you get the time to get into the mood of that particular song and give your best to it. The disadvantage could be that the album won't sound continuous, it might sound a bit broken up.

Sally: You had the foresight, when you started, to get your own company together so that you were totally in charge of everything. Where did you get that business sense from?

Kate: Well, although that was my decision, the advice came from the people around me which is continually the situation. It often sounds much bigger than it is, me being the head of the management company. What it means is I say yes or no ultimately, which is what I want because it's my life.

I was in a unique situation when I started because I had absolutely no one looking after me apart from a few people at E.M.I. and my solicitor, and it remained that way until I was a success. I was, in fact, successful without any kind of management at all.

Sally: So you negotiated your deal with E.M.I. yourself?

Kate: Yes, with my father and my solicitors. I really don't think E.M.I. knew how to handle it which is why in many ways the thing was held back for years. But it was good; it was what I needed. I really wanted to make an album more than anything but I realised they weren't getting in contact and nothing was actually happening. Rather than just hanging round at home all day not doing anything except writing songs I thought I'd take up something to get me out into the world and to help the music. I thought the obvious thing was dancing. So I started going to dance and mime classes and I was going up to London so much it really meant I had to move from my parents. So in all this time a lot was happening to me and in a way I think I knew that I was planning a stronger foundation for myself because I was still a kid and I needed to grow up pretty quick.

Sally: When you started dancing classes, did you go thinking that you might want to interpret your song with dance or did that come because of the classes?

Kate: I knew that that was what I wanted to do. I saw Lindsay Kemp in 'Flowers' and I knew that I'd seen something that was incredibly important to my direction from there on. He wasn't opening his mouth, none of them were, yet the amount of emotion they were creating was something I'd never seen in any other dance theatre or by actors or singers. I felt if there was any way to combine that with music then I'd be able to express to people the sort of emotion I wanted. I went to his classes with that in mind, and from his classes to other people's classes and at one point it nearly got to where I thought of giving up my music to become a dancer. I loved it so much, it seemed to have more purpose sometimes. I was training very intensely doing three or four hours a day. I'm not training like that any more. I realised it wasn't where my priorities were, that the music was the priority and then it all seemed to make sense that it was music and dance.

Sally: But you started writing when you were eleven. Where did the ideas for writing come from? It's quite unusual for people of that age to actually write songs.

Kate: Yes. I think a lot of it might have been to do with the things inside me and realising how much pleasure music had given to other people I'd seen. Maybe it was because I had to play alone a lot.

Sally: Were you quite a solitary child then?

Kate: I had no friends of my own age until I went to school and those friends lived quite a way from me. And my brothers, who were a bit older than me, were out doing other things.

Sally: So you had to amuse yourself?

Kate: I spent a lot of time by myself.

Sally: Success happened very quickly. How equipped were you to cope with it?

Kate: I think a lot of the things I'd done really helped me. Like the whole thing of dancing and the humiliation when you can't dance; you learn a lot inside. You learn to build up certain things and to realise that you're not shit hot. It's very good for you. I think it gave me a pretty strong internal foundation to build on. I was just dying to do another album. That first album meant everything to me and in a way it started with the album for me rather than the single because the single came off the top.

Sally: Do you ever worry that you are going to run out of ideas?

Kate: Yes. The main thing that really worries me is that some of our songs stick and that's really scary because the song is the initial creation. If you've got a song then all those ideas within that song can be turned into a video and a dance routine. The song is what everything else comes from. Sometimes I get really worried that I'm drying up, especially when I'm working hard and I'm tired and I'm not working on creative things. I start thinking, 'Who am I? What am I doing? I should be writing instead of talking about myself or being in front of cameras.' You really start to doubt your purposes.

Sally: So if you lock yourself away, does it start to happen?

Kate: Yeah. I need to be alone and I need to have time to think, so what I do now is spend as much time as possible creating, then I set a whole time aside for general promotion and of course I do odd things in between. I do all the stuff to be done on the business level at one point in the year then that way I've got all the rest for promotional activity.

As far as I'm concerned when you do an album and you put a lot of work into it and it's got a lot of good people on it you should at least go and talk to people about it, letting people know it's born. Apart from that, I don't really feel I should sit and talk to people about myself.

Sally: What about live performances? Are you thinking of going out again?

Kate: I really want to do another show, I really do. What I don't want to do is to start planning for a show and not get the album done in time. I know this has happened to some people and their shows have been a disaster because they've had to rush into them. Though I would like to do a show now I feel I need another album's worth of material.

Sally: I should think it's going to be very hard to follow the acclaim you had for your last shows. Does that worry you?

Kate: Not really because in so many ways that was an embryo of things that could happen. It was a big experiment as far as I was concerned. I just slung a load of ideas together with links and colours and hoped that it would work. I think we could do so much more than we did because we were relying quite a lot on props. I feel ideally that as much of the performance as possible should be human: it shouldn't all be huge gimmicks. I have a lot more dance ideas.

Sally: You took several months getting that together so presumably you'd have to spend several months preparing the next one?

Kate: Yes. It should be cut down a little because some of the things have been covered, but it's always going to take that amount of time because you've got the band to rehearse and you've got to fit the dance into the band; it's like piecing a jig-saw together.

Sally: You did a whole keep-fit campaign before you went out on tour, didn't you?

Kate: I had to, otherwise I wouldn't have been able to get through the show. When you're singing and dancing you have to breathe twice as much to be able to do it and even on the first week of the tour I was still trying to learn how to handle it. What you do is learn points in the show where you do everything you can to get your breath back, then you can let it all hang out for the next two numbers.

Sally: How did you get fit?

Kate: Well, lots of training. The incredible thing was that during the rehearsal periods I was getting three or four hours' sleep a night and then dancing in the morning plus a band rehearsal, then I'd have a costume meeting or something. It was just ridiculous. We went straight from that rehearsal period into the tour. That's a problem because you literally reach an exhaustion point by about the end of eight weeks on tour because you've been going for those few months before it started.

Sally: Were you totally exhausted by the end of it?

Kate: I was just blown away. Also something like that means so much to you that when it's suddenly gone there's nothing left of you – you're just an empty shell and you think, 'God, I want to do something but what can I do?' You find you try to write songs and you can't. It's all been taken away. You've put out so much that it's all gone and you literally have to let people give it back to you. My creative spirit didn't come back for quite a time.

Sally: Are you a person who's into keep fit and looking after yourself?

Kate: No, I'm not really. I don't tend to look after myself that well. I try but I'm not very good, especially with things like diets. When I'm working I'll often not have a meal. I'll have a bar of chocolate to give me some sugar and I'll drink loads of tea. I don't get enough sleep and I smoke cigarettes. I'm a vegetarian, not because I want to look after myself, but because the thought of eating animals just does me in.

Sally: Are you totally wrapped up in the business or do you have time for any private life at all?

Kate: No, I'm not really wrapped up in the business. I don't go to do's or anything as I'd much rather be working. I do get a fair amount of private life because at the moment I'm in the studio and as most of my friends are musicians, they come and see me which is lovely. I don't really get that much time but it's O.K. because what I like doing is what I *am* doing.

Sally: Do you see yourself getting married and having children?

Kate: Not really. I love children. I think they're fantastic and the thought of actually having a child of one's own is incredible, but I have no urge for that as yet.

Sally: What are the most special things that have happened?

Kate: There have been some really lovely things. Working with Roy Harper on his album and working with Peter Gabriel – they really mean a lot to me.

Sally: What about your songs? Is there one that means more to you than the others?

Kate: The one that was really special for me was 'Breathing' because so many different energies went into that song and came out of it. It nearly made me cry, that backing track; the musicians had been trying so hard to get the track but it was the second day and they just weren't playing it with enough feeling. Then all of a sudden, all this feeling came out. The bass was singing and the drums really meant it. We went in to listen. I just wanted to cry, it was so beautiful, and from that point everything just seemed to go right.

PHIL COLLINS

We unfortunately upset Phil Collins when he last appeared on 'Tiswas'. On the previous occasion we'd pelted him with pies, as is our wont, but this time we treated him with the respect he deserved: I interviewed him, we played the promotion film for 'In the Air Tonight' and set a competition. All very genteel. But the following week his record company promotion man rang me and said, 'Phil's upset that he didn't get a custard pie'. Well, I realise we can't go upsetting top stars like him, so I'll arrange a good flanning for him during the next series.

I went to Phil's house to interview him for the book. It's certainly a beautiful spot and very peaceful. In fact, it's so quiet you can hear the grass grow. It must be lovely when life is going well but very lonely if it isn't. It seemed an ideal place for him to lock himself away and create all those marvellous hits!

Sally: Phil, you've had tremendous solo success. Has it made you feel you'd like to pursue a solo career and perhaps leave Genesis?

Phil: No. I think it's made me consider everything I do from where I am now as opposed to being a member of a band trying to do other things. Suddenly I feel like an individual. Rather than having to collaborate with people to get something done. I can either do things on my own or dabble in a lot of other things, and one of those things that I choose to dabble in is Genesis, although dabble isn't really the right word.

Sally: How does that work within the structure of the band?

Phil: Well, Mike and Tony have done their own albums, but they've never been the types to go out and play with other people. The only reason they're in a group at all is because no one else played their music. It's not as if they wanted to be in a group and to write. They wrote music first and foremost and then, because they couldn't find anybody to play with them, they ended up having to go on the road. This is like ten years ago. Their attitude towards music is different from mine. I came into the business from the playing point of view, and that carries on; I always play with other people. Even after a Genesis tour I find it relaxing to go and play with somebody else as opposed to sitting down and doing nothing. What I've just said about me is an unwritten and unsaid rule. If you said that to Tony or Mike they'd say, 'Well, I don't think like that. I was hoping that Phil would still see the band as most important.' I do see it as important but . . .

Sally: As part of the overall thing?

Phil: Yes. Maybe it's different because I've had success with my thing and Tony and Mike have had small success.

Sally: How much time a year would you devote to Genesis?

Phil: Well, at the moment I'm still devoting as much time as necessary. We work things out pretty much in advance. We decided that after my record we'd go in to rehearse an album, write it and then see how long it takes. I've been working on it since November. Then we pick up the pieces again and start rehearsing for the road. I guess this year has been one of the more busy years of Genesis in terms of staying together – six months.

Sally: How many people do you take on the road with you?

Phil: It varies. 1978 was a ridiculous year. I was still meeting people at the end of the tour that I'd never met, yet they'd been with us for six months! There were about fifty people on that tour because it was like building a house every day. We had six ten by ten mirrors, they weren't actually mirrors, they were reflectives, but they were pretty heavy stuff. It was all worked by computers. They'd all go in unison and lights would come up and reflect off them so it looked symmetrical. We were playing lots of big gigs and it looked very nice from a long way away if you couldn't see the group. It was a huge big show with lasers and all that stuff.

Sally: It must've cost a fortune.

Phil: It did. We lost a lot of money that year and also, you felt part of a machine. So we decided to forget about all that and that's why last year we did the English tour and just did theatres. We had a very small crew by comparison. We stripped the whole show down; we didn't have any hardware apart from the lighting rig and I think it was good value. We just thought we'd play small places where we had eye to eye contact.

Sally: Let's go back to your solo album for a minute. Had the idea to do a solo album been in your head for a long time?

Phil: No, it just literally crept up behind me! I'd never really finished songs; I'd written bits, given them to Genesis and let the band muck about with them, but here I was with a lot of time and I was actually finishing songs, or if I didn't finish them, I wanted to carry on until I had. And over a period of a year and a half to two years I had accumulated all these tapes. By this time I'd said to Mike and Tony, 'I'm going to Vancouver to try and patch things up. If I don't come back, "Bye"'. So they said, 'Don't rush it,' and they'd do their solo albums. When I came back ready to work they were in the middle of their thing so I had to do something. That's when I started writing. At the same time, Brand X went over the budget so we came down to the house one day to do one of their tracks. We didn't have any more money to go to the studio so we thought, 'Let's forget about the studio. Let's do it upstairs and see how it works.' So we did it, then we took the eight-track tape to a studio and transferred it to twenty-four tracks and then carried on over-dubbing. It cost us nothing and the result which had been got upstairs was no different really from the result that we'd got in the studio. I thought if that was true then all the stuff that I'd been doing upstairs could, in theory, be an album or backing tracks for an album. Before I knew it, I'd accumulated all this material and I had an album. There was never a point when I said, 'Now I'm going to do my record.' I'd never have wanted to do that anyway.

Sally: Didn't you give 'In the Air Tonight' to the group at one stage?

Phil: Yes. When we did 'Duke' we actually rehearsed it. Everyone came in with their tapes and I played what I had and they played me what they had and there were certain things that they liked. 'Misunderstanding' was going to be on my album but they liked it and also 'Please Don't Ask'. I remember playing them 'Missed Again' and 'In the Air' and 'If Leaving Me is Easy. Of course, they didn't sound like the album versions. 'In the Air' and 'Missed Again' didn't sound far off but 'If Leaving Me is Easy' needed a bit of imagination and they didn't like it as it was; not didn't like it, but they wouldn't have done it as simply as I would have liked.

Sally: Tell me about your audition for Genesis.

Phil: I looked at Melody Maker and saw this advert which had a box round it: all adverts in boxes are usually pretty good jobs. It said 'Drummer, sensitive to acoustic music, 12-string guitarist/lead guitarist wanted for a group, Stratton-Smith'. I'd known Tony Stratton-Smith for years so I thought I'd just ring Strat up and get the job easy. I didn't even know what group it was. Strat said, 'It's really down to Peter, Tony and Mike. I can't give you the job, you've got to audition.'

So I went down to Peter's parent's farm which was

pretty luxurious with a swimming-pool in the back garden.

There were lots of drummers before me so Peter said, 'Have a swim while you're waiting.' I did and I could hear the other drummers auditioning. They were going through a routine with quiet bits, loud bits, soft bits, dramatic bits and acoustic bits to test out the blokes' versatility. I heard it three or four times before it was my go. I'm pretty quick in terms of remembering things, but when I went in there to play I made it look a bit hard! As you know, I got the job!

Sally: That's eleven years ago. Do you see Genesis going on and on?

Phil: Well, I know some people will groan, but I can't see why not. I really think the band will keep on going until it gets it right. That's my attitude towards it.

Sally: How far off is that?

Phil: I don't know. It gets better with each album, but it's never quite right. I guess when there's three individuals in the group who have strong ideas, you all try and lean each other towards what you want it to be. It doesn't cause friction. We don't argue at all. We have disagreements about musical things but usually we see sense and the person who sees sense the most wins. Genesis music is full of grand chords and is very romantic. My side of things isn't like that. Mike's writing isn't like that but Tony's writing is and he's trying to get out of it. He's finding it hard to because of the kind of person he is. Mike and I are trying to get him out of it and he's trying too. Mike's also trying to change and I'm trying to do different things. It's like we're all struggling to try and change the band. We're getting there gradually and I think 'Duke' is an improvement on anything else that we've done in terms of being less what people expect from us. If you ask someone if they like Genesis, most people, apart from our real fans, will say no. If they say no it's usually because they heard stuff maybe three or four or five years ago and they didn't like it. They liked my record, which is very gratifying, but I find myself constantly discovering that people didn't hear 'Duke'. When you think that we do an album a year, if you didn't hear 'Duke' then you haven't really heard Genesis for three years. A lot of water goes under the bridge and I feel we're much maligned, but you know, my basic reason for staying in Genesis is to try and get it right. I think that this new form is going to surprise people in terms of the kind of music it is.

Sally: It sounds as if you're having a lot more influence over this album.

Phil: Well, I have got a lot more energy. 'Duke' was the first album really when I didn't have to come home to a family and so I was the first to get to the studio and the last to leave. Before 'Duke' I worked with Peter on his album, although I'm not claiming anything apart from playing some good drums. Some of the ideas that were floating around influenced me a lot – the sparseness, the way to record things by not using too many instruments. It was a bit like coming out of a cloud. When we came to do 'Duke' I had a lot of energy for it and for the band and that was the first album I could say I was 99% pleased with. An album takes real commitment. With Clapton, for instance, who's a neighbour and a mate of mine, he leaves his responsibility at the studio door. He records his music and he lets somebody else produce it. To me that's like a painter saying to somebody else, 'Will you put a bit of blue up there?' In theory, producing should be an extension or an explanation of what you're doing. I don't really want to be involved in anything where I can't actually say, 'Well, this is as much me as I could possibly get it.' There's no alternative for me but to put everything I've got into it. With the Genesis album I'm trying to make it something I can be as proud of as possible.

Sally: You mentioned that you were going to be working with Pete Townshend during the summer. What are you going to be doing with him?

Phil: He rang me up when his last solo album was being made and, in fact, when Moon died I actually rang him up and said, 'Listen, is there anything I can do? I'll gladly lend my services because I've always wanted to play with the Who.' I love Townshend as a bloke. He's one of the few pop people who've really handled themselves with integrity and he seems to be a really 'spot on' bloke. Anyway, his office rang me back and said, 'Could you come down?' and I thought, 'I'm gonna play'. As it happened he wanted me to play on a session he was producing which was fine because I got a chance to meet him. We got on very well and from there, he wanted me to play on his solo album.

Sally: But if you'd played with the Who, as you say you'd like to have done, would you have considered working for them full time?

Phil: Well yes, probably. At that time I just thought, 'Well, I do Brand X and Genesis; I could do the Who, Brand X and Genesis.'

Sally: You really think you could have done all that?

Phil: Yes. At that time, they were just making albums and doing a few gigs. Had I said to Genesis, 'I'm doing the Who's tour,' I am sure that something could have been worked out and we could have started our album later.

Sally: Does going off and doing other things give you new ideas?

Phil: Sure, yes. I'd feel very claustrophobic if I just had the one thing.

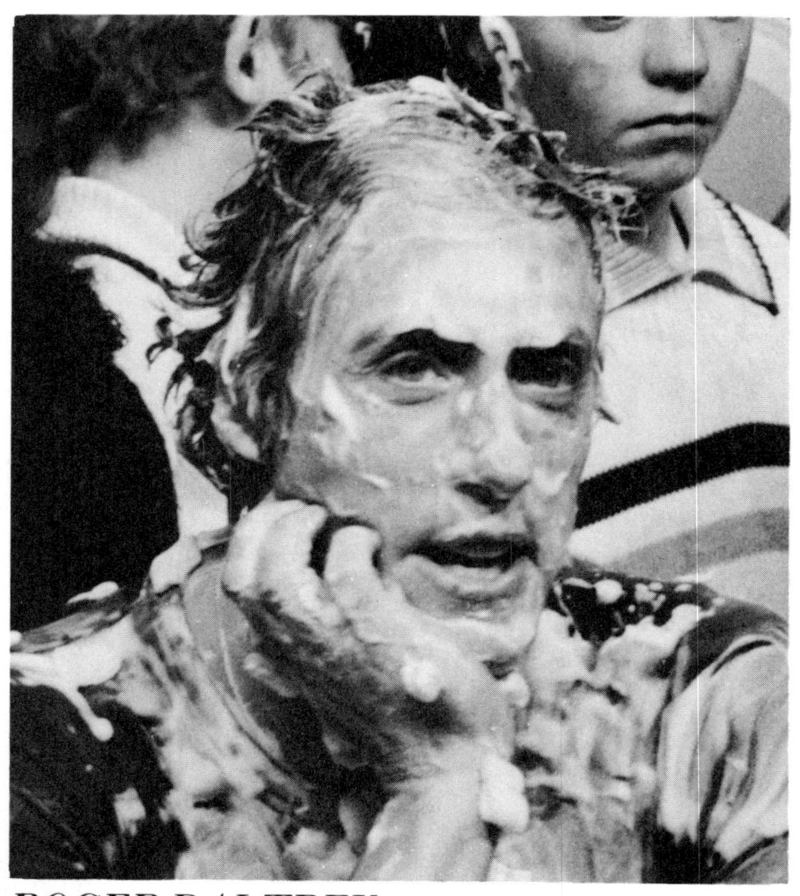

ROGER DALTREY

Roger invited me down to his home in the heart of the countryside for our interview. He owns a beautiful house and most of Sussex (400 acres to be precise.)
He was rather unhappy about the freezing cold water we'd thrown at him when he'd appeared on 'Tiswas'. Apparently, once whilst filming, Ken Russell had kept him standing in water all day and since then Roger can't bear cold water! He was relieved to hear that with the 1981-82 series we would be celebrating the year of the pie.

Sally: So here we are, in the middle of nowhere. Do you like to be completely cut off?

Roger: I always wanted to live in the country, right from the start. Even when I was five years old I used to run away to the country, which was the bomb site up the road! I always promised myself that if I ever made any money I'd get the hell out of London, and here I am. I don't like being cut off from people. I'm not really cut off. I've just opened up a trout fishery, so I get all the fishermen coming.

Sally: Do you fish?

Roger: I used to – it's wonderful therapy. But now I've started building the fishery I don't get time any more. I just watch everybody else and take the money.

Sally: You've also got the farm going, haven't you?

Roger: Yes. Farming is a bit of a disaster at the moment. In fact it's terrible. I just don't understand how farmers earn a living because there's absolutely no money in it at all. The only money you're making really is that your land is going up in value, but again, in the last two years it's gone down in value.

Sally: Trout fishing, farming, all that apart, are you doing any other work?

Roger: We may have a film later on this year. It's this monocled mutineer thing. This mad confidence trickster – a true story of a mutiny in the British Army in the First World War. They're still trying to get it made this year but it might go into next year.

Sally: You and the rest of the group own Shepperton Studios. Are you planning to do anything with that?

Roger: We haven't got the money to do it. When we bought that and Keith was alive, it was easy. Keith died, and it threw a great big spanner in the works because his estate takes all his quarter out so it's milking the company dry. It was great when there were four of us. It's not good with three of us. It doesn't work any more.

Sally: So what are you going to do with it?

Roger: We don't know. It's a wonderful white elephant! At least we don't have small ones. I mean – a film studio

– we couldn't have something simple! It costs so much money to make films. The two films that we did make, we borrowed the money from Polydor, and even though the films themselves actually earned as much money as we borrowed, by the time they added their interest on, over the period it took to make the film, we'll never ever pay it back. It's a joke. It's all a joke. And they were very successful. 'Quadrophenia' and 'McVicar' made a lot of money, but it's like a rat trap – you get in it and there's no way out.

Sally: Groupwise, what are the plans?

Roger: We're going to reform. After breaking up for the 3,000th time, or so it says in the papers. I kept reading we were breaking up. It's amazing what they wrote about our tour because I thought we'd done the best shows we'd ever done and so did the fans. It looked to me as if they refused to send writers down that liked the Who.

I found it absolutely unbelievable. For instance, the last shows we did were in London, at Wembley, and the audience was on its feet from start to finish and they were great. They were good shows. I'm not just saying that – our standards are high but they were good shows, there was nothing bad about them, and the reviews we read I couldn't believe. I just wondered whether they went to the same show. The audience was standing from the first second, right until the end, and you don't keep an audience doing that for two hours if it's a bad show.

Sally: What about this story that we all read about the Who splitting up. That surprised you as well, did it?

Roger: Yes. That came after we did a really bad show at the Rainbow. My wife had just had a baby and I was getting the kids up for school, and I wasn't into being a rock and roll star. When you get on stage with the band you have to change. I don't particularly like the character that gets on there, but that's what you have to do, and that night I just couldn't do it. For the first time in my career, I was just somewhere else. I just wasn't into it. It just so happens that when we usually have problems, the rest of the band rallies round and helps out. It happened that night Pete was 'tired as a newt' (laughter) and, of course, when I was out there looking for help there was none to be given. It was a disastrous show. And then I read in the papers about this huge argument and the bust up. It wasn't even an argument. It was quite funny to read all these lies. But then, it went on for too long and started getting serious.

In America we're enormous, but we do cater for the American market. Since '72 we've concentrated on making albums and we've played mostly in America and neglected England. England has always been a singles market. We want to become a big band again, not that we're small now, but if we want to become as popular as a lot of these new bands we just have to make ourselves available to the market that's there. That means making singles and playing England more. I want to do another tour of England now. I want to see what they're going to write about us. It can't get any worse. I think that's what we should do.

Sally: Do you find then that you don't enjoy the touring and making albums merry-go-round as much as you did in the early days?

Roger: No, I love it. I mean, I like going on stage and playing and I like going in the studio for a couple of hours and coming out with a record, but I can't for the life of me stand going in a studio for a year and coming out with one album. To me that is just not rock 'n' roll. The last Who album took nine months to do. But my bit of it took about a week. I think it should be more instant. To me pop music was always recorded today and released tomorrow and, if you like, forgotten about a week later, until say a couple of years later when you say, 'That was good'. And that's how quick it should be, but everybody's so conscious of it now; there's something about it that isn't as bright as it used to be.

Sally: So your involvement with an album is just to go in and sing. You're not there for the rest of it?

Roger: Well, not the way they record, no. I don't want to be there. I just get bored with it. By the time I get to sing on it I'm so bored with it I can't even sing. It's true. Unless you're working, unless you're producing or playing an instrument, who wants to sit around in a recording studio all day for nine months?'

Sally: What about your solo albums? It's been a while now, since you made one, hasn't it?

Roger: It was only a hobby. There's nothing I want to do at the moment. When I started, I found Leo Sayer. He was having terrible trouble getting anyone to listen to his songs and I thought it would be good to sing someone else's songs. I'd only ever sung Townshend's songs. So I did that first album and it really worked well for Leo and got his career off the ground. A good stepping stone anyway, and it was good for me as a singer. Then I did a soully disco album and then I did a kind of nowhere album – I didn't have any direction. I just went in. I was under contract to do an album and I had to come up with something and I wasn't really in the mood. But everybody was a lot more serious about it than I ever was. They were still quite successful. I'm not complaining.

Sally: What about song writing? Do you ever get involved in that at all?

Roger: Oh, I'm terrible. I can't write to save my life. I mean, I can write average songs – but think of the kind of lyrics I've been singing for all these years. They're so good it makes you feel a bit inferior. I know you shouldn't worry about that, but you can't help but feel it.

Sally: People do often say it's now Pete Townshend's Who, don't they? Does that bug you?

Roger: It isn't at all. They say that, but they don't know anything about it. It isn't at all. I think the last album was Pete Townshend's Who. I was very unhappy with it.

Sally: What were you unhappy about?

Roger: It had no balls.

Sally: Do the group know how you feel?

Roger: Yes, I told them. I think the reviews were very honest about it, saying, '. . . a session man singing Peter Townshend's songs'. That's the way the album was produced and that's how we were all treated.

Sally: Do you think with the next one you might get more involved as it goes along to make sure it's more how you'd want it to be?

Roger: I went to see him about it last week. It has to work both ways. Pete has to be prepared to take a bit more criticism of his songs in the making and we have to get a producer who allows it to go on like that. We didn't have that. It was a bit of a disaster.

Sally: When you first started it took a long time for you all to actually earn any money, didn't it? You seemed to be heavily in debt for a long time. Was that because of the expensive touring or the expensive life style?

Roger: It certainly wasn't the life style. It was a terrible life style – I lived in the back of a truck for four years. The only one who made any money was Townshend because he was writing the songs. The group was footing the bill for all his ranting and ravings on stage. When he was smashing up guitars at £1,000 a time, we were earning £200 a night. Of course, one day someone added up the figures and, God, it all came out in incredibly bright red ink. Then, we were £60 - £90,000 down, really in the red. We had nothing, no hopes of ever paying it back. That was a lot of money then. That was about the equivalent now of £¾ million. We used to have accounts meetings and we used to laugh – we couldn't do anything else. We used to sit around laughing at these incredible figures and the accountant would be crying, saying, 'I'm serious'. There was nothing you could do. It becomes so ridiculous that you have to laugh.

Sally: You managed to pay it off?

Roger: 'Tommy' became very successful and we made a lot of money.

Sally: Was it not until then that you had any money?

Roger: Yes, not until then. 1968. Well, that came out in '68 but we didn't get the money till 1970. We've only had money for ten years. And it's nice to have it. No matter what they ever say about it, there's nothing that's bad about it.

Sally: How long can you see the Who rocking on for?

Roger: Don't know. I like our energy thing. We can rock on for as long as Peter Townshend wants to, to be honest with you. It's down to him because if he doesn't want to do it then there's no point. So it's up to him, really.

Sally: Were he to suddenly say he'd had enough and knock the whole thing on the head, you would presumably pursue your acting career?

Roger: Yes, or work on my trout farm, I just don't care about it that much. It's not worth worrying about. To me the only reason you go out there is because you *all* want to be out there doing it. If one of you doesn't want to be there, there's no point in any of you being there. We've had this problem with Pete for years and it's really boring; he seems to want to play with everybody else – really weird. I just hope he sorts himself out. But if he doesn't want to do it, it doesn't bother me. It will upset me if the Who's all over because it's been a great career, but it won't be the end of my life.

Sally: Does Pete just get fed up with the whole thing?

Roger: I don't know. Pete gets fed up with Pete, that's the trouble. Like I say, I just wish he'd make up his mind what he does want because there's nothing worse than getting on a stage full of people and finding that one of them doesn't really want to be there. It's a horrible feeling.

Sally: But do you tend to force him out on the road?

Roger: I have done in the past but I'm not doing it any more. I give up. I don't mean that negatively. I said to him the other day, 'If you want it to stop, Pete, that's fine by me.' It doesn't bother me any more. I thought if we had packed up when Keith died, that would have been tragedy on tragedy.

Sally: And you were thinking of doing that?

Roger: He was. I wasn't. I'm not thinking of packing up now. I've never been one for easy ways out. I like to keep fighting for things and I still think we're one of the best bands around.

Sally: So was it your influence over the others to carry on after Keith died?

Roger: Yeah.

Sally: Was it you that found Kenny?

Roger: That was Pete. To be really honest, and it might cause a lot of trouble and a lot of arguments and it might sound like I'm being back biting, but I wouldn't have had anybody. I would have kept it to the three members that were left, and I would have had a drummer for one tour and one album, and then another drummer because to me it was stupid trying to replace Keith. It sounds terrible to say this but the one good thing about Keith dying is that it did free the Who of all its problems, all its chains. We could have done anything. And then we go and lumber ourselves with another drummer. I didn't want to do that, I wanted to keep the door open and never sign anyone up. Just use people, just get people in, mates in one week and out the next – so we'd feel free. I think it was a great mistake getting a drummer. So there.

Sally: You don't all sit down and make a democratic decision by the sound of things.

Roger: It was Pete Townshend's Who then. I just wanted to keep him happy so that he'd go on the road.

Sally: A trade off?

Roger: Well, it is really. Now, I won't do any more. I've discovered the one thing that doesn't work with Pete Townshend is to give him his own way. He doesn't know what he wants for a start. I regretted the drummer thing. I still do. Kenny's good, but I think of the things that might have been.

SHEENA EASTON

Sheena is one of those people who lights up a room when she walks into it. I got to know her quite well after her first 'Tiswas' appearance when we shared a long train journey from Birmingham to London. She endeared herself to me forever when she suggested we while away the time playing cribbage (one of my favourite pastimes). Mind you, we would have been drummed out of any decent card school because of our incessant chatter.

Sheena managed to demolish almost a box of chocolates handed to her by a fan as she stepped on the train, but read on about how she's given all that up.

Sally: I gather you've been on a huge keep fit campaign.

Sheena: Yes, I haven't had any chocolates for three weeks. I've been drinking milk and taking lots of vitamin tablets.

Sally: Do you feel any better?

Sheena: No.

Sally: So will you go back to the old routine?

Sheena: Actually, I was a glutton for sweets. I was constantly eating sweets, especially when working on the road.

Sally: I know, I remember.

Sheena: I'd have three Mars Bars a day because I often don't have time for dinner and by the time you've done a gig you're too shattered. I'm also a cereal fiend. Sometimes all I'd have in a day was three bowls of cornflakes, a couple of Mars Bars, and maybe an orange or something. That isn't good for you. So I thought, 'Right, cut all this out. Start being sensible.'

Sally: So you thought you'd do that to get fitter.

Sheena: Yeah, and I bought all these vitamins for nervous exhaustion, vitamins for my nails . . . I'm taking five vitamin tablets three times a day.

Sally: You look very fit and you've just come back from Japan which must have been exhausting.

Sheena: The trip was very successful because the album, when we left, was at number five and the two singles were in the charts. All that side of it was fine, but it was really exhausting. I don't know if I really enjoyed it. It was total work. There was a press conference with over 100 photographers and 300 journalists. You have to handle all that, then you have two television shows in a day, then a business dinner at night – and this was every day! It was just exhausting. I went to Australia, too, and I loved that. We worked hard, but it didn't seem as punishing. Japan was just exhausting.

Sally: Now America is going well for you. How did you enjoy your first trip there?

Sheena: I loved it because I find the Americans' attitude very pro. In any country you go to there's always one person who's negative. Some journalist or whatever. There, nobody knocked, not one person. That seems to be the American mentality; they're all for success and all for encouraging you. The only thing with America as opposed to Britain is that there are a lot of people who are insincere. They say everything is wonderful. It took a while to find out the sincere ones and ones who were just over the top all the time.

Sally: You went off to Montserrat to do the first album and you're going to Caribou in Colorado for the next one. Do you like to get out of England to record?

Sheena: We needed the break. We'd just done the first tour and we were all exhausted. I thought, 'Great, an excuse for a holiday', but it was surprising because we did more work than we would have done if we'd been in England. We got the whole album done in two weeks.

Sally: How much say do you have in what's recorded? Is it between you and Chris Neal, your producer?

Sheena: It's between me and Chris, but Chris listens to everything and filters it. I've got sixty cassettes lying on my bedroom floor and out of that we pick about ten tracks. We met yesterday and decided on the tracks, then we got a phone call today saying we've got new songs in, so we're going back today to decide more. Generally I rely very heavily on his judgement.

Sally: One of the marketing managers here at EMI has told me they don't think there's anyone that's ever broken so quickly all over the world. Has it changed you at all in any way that you're aware of?

Sheena: I keep saying I haven't changed, but I suppose everybody changes. I'm a different person now than when I was a drama student of nineteen, but I don't think I've changed drastically. I've got two really close friends that I've lived with for the past year; they don't think I've changed and they're my barometers. My outlook hasn't changed. In a way I have changed because now the central point of my life is my work. It's the whole point of my life. I don't have time for a great deal of social life.

Sally: Does that bother you?

Sheena: It bothers me only if I'm not working. When I'm working I never think of my social life.

Sally: Do you mind that the press is so interested in your private life?

Sheena: Yes, I mind that a lot. I don't mind if they're interested because we're all nosey. If there's a piece of paper with writing on it lying on a desk we'll read it. But if I said, 'I'd rather you didn't read that,' you'd have no right to demand to. Well, I don't like the demands of some people who, whenever you say, 'I don't want to discuss that,' get all upset and huffy and think, 'How dare she not discuss that'. That's what annoys me; that can get me angry at times. If you categorically say, 'No comment. That's my own private life. I don't want to talk about it', they all think there must be a skeleton there. I don't have any skeletons. I wish I had; my private life's too boring. If I had a troop of ten journalists living in my flat to write about anything they heard going on, it would be boring reading, I can assure you. The other thing that gets me is that they're always trying to link you with someone. They see you with somebody and they think it's the big romance. You can't have friendships.

Sally: Back to your career. You've said that you think you would have made it without the 'Big Time'. How would you have gone about doing it?

Sheena: I wouldn't have made it so soon without the 'Big Time' because that was more than a step up the ladder; it was like I was catapulted up it. I've got lots of friends in the business that I was in drama college with and they all think they're going to be stars. You need to think that. I was at drama college and singing with a band and I'd made up my mind that I was going into singing and that I was going to come down to London, join a band and do the pub gigs. I had an idea of trying to get into session singing, plus work in a band, and that way if some producer liked my voice I'd get a recording contract. It's naïve, but then I was a nineteen-year-old kid in Glasgow and that's how I thought it was done. I also had the idea of investing some money and making some good demo tapes and then just flogging them constantly round the record companies. And I was a fiend for auditioning as well.

Sally: Yes. You pretended you were twelve years old once, didn't you, for 'Annie'?

Sheena: Yes, and before I auditioned for the 'Big Time', I was going to audition for 'Evita', but I went to audition for the 'Big Time' instead.

Sally: Did they tell you straight away or did they keep you on tenterhooks?

Sheena: When I went down and met Esther she said, 'The idea is that we're going to choose six girls out of all these auditions and send them to EMI to audition.' Obviously they couldn't make a programme unless they got a girl who could get a recording contract. They'd already chosen a couple of girls. After I'd been interviewed and sung for Esther she said she was really interested. I went home to Glasgow and I got a phone call the next day from the director asking if I wanted the show. I said, 'Do you mean do I want the audition for EMI along with the six girls?' and he said, 'No, just you. We want you. It's up to you to get a recording contract now.'

Sally: When you were making the programme did you mind the way people talked about you while you were sitting there?

Sheena: Yes and no. When I watched it recently I just found it so funny. I found me funny because that was me two years ago. Let's just say I wasn't forced into doing it. I volunteered so I've no room for complaint. It was misleading because the documentary didn't even show my replies. For instance, I spent ten minutes replying to Lulu's manager but that was never shown. I did speak and we discussed things, but it made better television just to show the comments. They didn't want my answers to be shown. It didn't bother me listening to all the comments because, quite frankly, if someone had said to me, 'I think you're the best thing since Barbra Streisand', I wouldn't have believed it. Equally, if somebody said to me, 'I think you're the worst thing I've ever heard. You'll never make it. You're rubbish', as somebody did, I wouldn't believe that either. I went into it thinking, 'Well, forget what anybody says because everybody's got an opinion'.

Sally: Obviously everyone has critics and like you were saying, everyone's entitled to an opinion, but when you released your first album there were some critics saying you were a manufactured item. Did that upset you?

Sheena: No, because the sort of music papers that say that keep changing their minds. They're comics – better than the Beano or the Dandy. They're so funny, these papers, because they're so bad. They have no conviction. One minute they love Tom Snott's band and it's the best thing since sliced bread, then they have a hit record and they hate them. So no, they don't bother me. If any journalist that I respected, or more particularly, any critic that I respected ever said that, I'd think about it. But I know the truth and the public are beginning to see the truth. I don't have session singers doing my lead vocal, it's me does the vocal. Come along to a concert and you'll hear a live vocal sound. As for manufactured – everybody is manufactured. Every single record that's put out is manufactured in the sense that it's recorded, pressed in a machine and the sound is produced.

Sally: Who do you particularly admire?

Sheena: I've always admired Joni Mitchell and she's always current, although she's never in the top charts. I tend to listen to non pop music on my record player. I listen to Joni Mitchell, Barbra Streisand and Billy Joel, who are popular, but not trendy.

Sally: You've said in the past that the highlight of your career was the Royal Variety Show. Is that still the case?

Sheena: Since then, the highlight for me was my first tour I suppose careerwise the highlight's got to be the American number one. But then everything new is a highlight. For 'When He Shines' to get to number twelve was really special because it was the fifth single off the first album and I thought, 'You can't possibly have five hits'. It's almost embarrassing to have five singles on one album!

Sally: Everything is going so incredibly well, you must wonder if it can all last.

Sheena: I wonder what I'm going to have to do to pay for it. I'm not a deeply religious person. I don't go to church but I do believe in God and sometimes I think, 'Well, God, what's going to happen? Am I going to lose my legs or something?' I've had a lot of luck but I'm not scared of it all going away. If I'd one hit that went to number one all round the world then I'd be worried because I could be a one hit wonder.

Sally: You're obviously not that.

Sheena: No. I've started to carve out a career in America and Japan so I've got other territories to work on. The only thing I regret is it all happened now.

Sally: Why?

Sheena: Well, it's like keeping a strawberry tart in your fridge all day and looking forward to eating it at six o'clock. Once you've eaten it it's gone and you can't look forward to it. So sometimes I think, 'I wish this had happened when I was thirty, not twenty'.

Sally: I know what you mean. Maybe it would have been better if a couple of the other territories had been a bit slower to take to you.

Sheena: Yes, exactly. It would have been nice to have an American number one next year, but at the same time I'm not going to hand this one back.

Sally: Having achieved so much have you got an ambition?

Sheena: Oh yes, that's the dual thing. When I sit down and analyse it it's greed; it's greed to do more. I keep remembering the first tour. I get a kick out of touring so October and November I'm looking forward to because I'm on the road. Next year I want to do less travelling for promotion and more travelling that's actually concert stuff. I want to have a sellout American concert tour. Now that won't be this year because after one hit you don't sell concert tours. It takes at least three or four. I've been asked to tour this year, but you can't do everything within a year, so I'm thinking of doing Canada and Australia. America is going to be the last territory I tour in because I don't want it going off the back of one or two hits. I might blow it for the rest of the year or for the next five years for that matter. I want to build up to that and also, I don't have all that much experience. I realised after the first tour how much I had to learn.

DAVE EDMUNDS

I arrived at Dave Edmunds' house on a lovely summer's day. He was happily ensconced in front of the telly watching snooker. He proudly informed me that his wife was at the ante-natal clinic. They were both obviously excited at the prospect of bringing a baby rock and roller into the world.

Anyway, being the hospitable chap he is, Dave offered me an afternoon drink of a Bloody Mary – and I hereby issue a warning – his Bloody Mary's are enough to blow your head off. However, we still managed to have a conversation . . .

Sally: How old were you when you first became interested in music?

Dave: Well, let's see. When rock 'n' roll records started coming out in this country it was about '55. That would make me twelve.

Sally: Did you then decide that you would like to start learning to play?

Dave: Yes. There was skiffle around and things like that. My elder brother Geoff had a skiffle group and there was always a guitar around the house. So we just started from there really. I started playing in his band and then I started my own at about seventeen.

Sally: You taught yourself to play guitar listening to records that you liked – what was the first thing you learnt to play?

Dave: I think 'Sandstorm' by Johnny and the Hurricanes.

Sally: So you used to listen to a record and then try to work out how you could play it.

Dave: You figured a lot out by yourself just through sheer enthusiasm. With that amount of enthusiasm you don't need much tuition because you know what you want to do, you know what direction you're going in. You hear a sound on a record and you work it out for yourself if you're that interested and you're thirteen years old. You just work it out.

Sally: So having left school, you formed the Raiders who didn't have much success.

Dave: None whatsoever.

Sally: Did you have a proper job as well?

Dave: Well, I had several actually, and I wasn't very good at any of them. I think I had about twenty-nine jobs, but I didn't do very well, and then when I got to the age of about twenty-two I thought, 'Now, this is no good', so I went on a Government training course to become a motor mechanic. I did a six-month course and I loved it, every minute of it, and I got a job which was the only job I ever held down.

Sally: So the breakthrough came really when you had your first hit 'Sabre Dance'?

Dave: Yes, when John Peel played it. We did the B.B.C.

session for him and he played the record and it was obvious that he hadn't heard it before he played it on the air. It was the last record of the programme before they went over to newstime and he shouted to the engineer to rewind the tape because he wanted to hear it again. He upset all the programme schedules and everything; it all went chaotic and there were lots of letters written in asking who was this. It was a very weird thing to do; it wasn't very good actually, but it was very different – that was what John liked.

Sally: You didn't really follow up in that same vein with the group, did you? What happened after that?

Dave: Well, all of a sudden we were thrust into big venues and doing tours of Britain, whereas I was just used to having a job and going out in the evenings – being just a local band, which gives you licence to do almost anything. You can do lots of Beatle songs, you don't have to be original if you don't want to. All of a sudden we were thrust into that big-timer circuit. I remember we did the Lyceum once with Joe Cocker supporting before he actually made it, and I just didn't feel comfortable with a band at all. I thought, 'This is not for me'. I also thought, 'Touring is not for me', which I later found out was wrong because I loved it with Rockpile.

Sally: You spent a couple of years after the whole Love Sculpture thing went away getting more interested in studio work, didn't you?

Dave: Yes, well I was very lucky, you see. I was very fortunate that a friend of mine had a little mono studio (Rockfield) as well as a hundred-acre dairy farm. The dream we had was to one day turn it into a Tamla Motown or something, but we only had two little mono machines. The success of 'Sabre Dance' gave him and me some success and some money, so we started putting in some good machines, and the next thing I know there's an eight-track machine – which was as good as any studio had then – and a mixer, and all the proper microphones and things like that. I was able to just go ahead to my heart's content and learn how to make records, all by myself if I wanted. That's how a lot of my earlier stuff was done. I played all the instruments because there was no one else there.

Sally: Very lonely work though.

Dave: Yes, it did get a bit lonely. It was also quite rewarding listening to a playback which sounds like a band, not just someone who's put lots of instruments over each other.

Sally: How long did it take to do 'Baby I Love You'?

Dave: I reckon about 200 hours in all, but there was no pressure. I didn't have a record company. Even after 'I Hear You Knocking' there was no deal that I had to deliver an album or so much product by such and such a time. I just gave them the record and they put it out which kept me going for a bit. I was able to indulge really, it was just pure indulgence.

Sally: This ability to recreate other people's sounds was criticised by Pete Townshend at the time, wasn't it?

Dave: Yes. I did an album for RCA which contained 'Baby I Love You', an Everly Brothers song and some of the stuff I did for the 'Stardust' movie, which was supposed to be as much like the originals as possible. When I played it to Pete in the studio he said, 'All you're doing, Dave, is celebrating the music. Instead of getting on with it and doing something with it yourself, you're sort of faithfully recreating it all!' He was absolutely right, of course, like he always is – the bugger!

Sally: Did that set you thinking about starting to create your own sound, or did that come later.

Dave: Well the problem with that, you see, is my first vocation is not that of a songwriter. I must be the first to admit it. It used to worry me and I used to tear my hair out and things like that, but in the end I had to think, 'Well, you can do what you do, do it and that's it.' So as soon as I accepted that I found I was helping Nick Lowe write songs and I've done quite a few with him.

Sally: What about when you signed with Led Zeppelin's label, Swan Song?

Dave: Yes, I was very grateful to Robert Plant for that. I had the Rockfield deal but the deal ran out and I waited round for something to happen and it didn't. I was sitting round for about two years wondering.

Sally: There wasn't anybody pushing you, saying you ought to be doing something?

Dave: No. So I went back down and Kingsley, who owns Rockfield Studios, let me have some time and I was halfway through the 'Get It' album when Robert Plant phoned me up (he just lives down the road in Kidderminster) and he said, 'Can I come down to the studio?' He came down and we got pissed and all that and he offered me a deal, which was amazing. I signed to the label in two weeks.

Sally: And then presumably you started to have the pressures of having to get things out.

Dave: Not really. One thing I insisted on in the contract was, 'You are not going to make me play live. You're not going to put in the contract that I have to go on tour.' And they said, 'No, that's all right, You do whatever you want, Just make the records.' I thought, 'Wow, this is great!'

And about that time I got together with Nick – just before that I had produced a Brinsley Schwartz album, so I got to know Nick then. And then low and behold – forgive the pun – Nick and I decided to get a band together, just do a few gigs round London and see how it went, and it went very, very well.

Sally: So Nick got you back into performing again.

Dave: Yes, I suppose so. I mean, neither of us intended to. He was fed up with all those years with the Brinsleys. We just used to go out to a pub every night and we were talking about it and the drunker we got the more we talked about going back on the road. And then eventually we did those gigs in London at the Nashville; we did a month's residency at the Nashville and Swan Song said, 'Why don't you support Bad Company? They're going on a four month tour of America'. We thought, 'This is great. This is it', so we went and got fired after two weeks.

Sally: Why?

Dave: I'm not quite sure. I think we were having too much fun. Basically they had booked 18,000 - 20,000 seaters and, as the tour went on, they were not selling all the seats, which was probably their profit margin. They needed a heavier support band to draw the crowds.

Sally: So that was the beginning of Rockpile. Are you pleased with the whole way Rockpile worked looking back on it now?

Dave: Yes, it was an odd way to start a band. As I was saying, Nick and I never had any real ideas of going back on the road and forming a band and, as a result, he'd signed to CBS, while I was already signed on to Swan Song. But those four years were heaven. I loved it all – all that touring and hard work which I had never known before. I never knew it could be like that and I really enjoyed it.

Sally: What about now? You've said that Rockpile is disbanding. What's the reason behind that?

Dave: Well, it's a musical one really. We spent all those years doing solo albums. If Nick was doing his solo album we would all go into the studio and do Nick's album, then we would all go in and do my solo album, and when we came to do the Rockpile one there seemed to be a lacking of musical direction. Usually a band will get something that they are known by–a sound, a style –and then they go off and do solo ablums. We did it...

Sally: The other way round?

Dave: Yeah, and we found all of a sudden we were down to do an album and we thought, 'What shall we do on it?' I thought, 'I've got a few songs, just the sort of thing I do on my albums.' Nick said the same. So it seemed we had a few songs that were like Nick Lowe album tracks and a few songs that were like Dave Edmunds album tracks. There was no unified purpose and we didn't know what to do about it, and more to the point, we didn't have time. Really we should have been thinking about it over the four years. During that time I've been asked in interviews, 'What can we expect from a Rockpile album when it comes together?' 'Oh, I'm sure it will just work itself out.' That's all I could say, and I was sure it would, but it didn't. It just seemed a very confused album with an identity crisis.

Sally: So that's really why you thought you'd knock it on the head.

Dave: Yeah, we sat round in a pub a few weeks ago and we thought, 'Well here were are trying to get material for the next album, and it's becoming even more diverse. We thought, 'This doesn't sound like a rock 'n' roll band. It didn't sound like the Rockpile I know and love.' It wasn't as if there was a conflict of ideas. It wasn't as if Nick was saying, 'Well, we should be doing this" and I was saying, 'No, we should be doing that'. In fact, no one knew what the hell to do about anything. There was just a feeling of despair about it. The first album sold pretty well, but not as well as we thought it would. In the States the Rockpile album, 'Seconds of Pleasure' didn't actually add up to the sales of Nick's last album and my last album put together, and we thought, well, something's wrong here, and we didn't know what it was. So we thought we'd just split.

Sally: You must be unhappy about that though, after the four great years you've had.

Dave: Yes, but if I could have seen a way out of it and the split had still occurred I would have been unhappy. I just had to agree with Nick. He said, 'Let's quit while we are ahead.'

Sally: You're concentrating quite a bit on producing, aren't you?

Dave: Yes, that's a thing I never thought I would get into because I wasn't really enjoying it. It was good fun to gain experience so I could produce myself. And then the Stray Cats came along and I thought, 'This is my cup of tea, this is completely different.' Well, I thought I'd love to produce them, but I wouldn't approach them because everyone else was. When they started up, they said it was a hype, but it wasn't. It was just a lot of interest being shown by everyone in the business. The group asked me to produce them which I was very pleased to do.

Sally: What about the performing of your own stuff, going off and doing your own gigs?

Dave: I want to do that again. But I'd like to see it happen in the autumn. Summer is really too busy. I've got to finish off the Pole Cats' album, possibly some more Stray Cats' work, and there's another band in America who've asked me to produce them, which I am quite interested in. I don't have enough time for this summer, and then the baby's coming in September. I'll have to be home for that.

Sally: Yes, you must be; what about ambitions? Have you got any special ambition, something you particularly want to achieve?

Dave: Well actually, I've had quite a few hit singles over the years but I've never had a really big album and I would love to have a big album.

Sally: What about your rock and roll idols, who are they?

Dave: Shakin' Stevens at the moment. He always has been ever since I produced his first album in '71. But from the old guys I suppose it was just the giants who influenced me. I'm not going to come up with any obscure names who made their records in a potato loft in Arkansas or something. It's Gene Vincent, Carl Perkins, Jerry Lee Lewis, Elvis Presley, the Everly Brothers especially, just those.

Sally: Are there any songs that you haven't done yet, any more of the old rock 'n' roll classics that you think you'd like to do?

Dave: I don't think I should do that. I've done quite a bit of it, and I think rock 'n' roll classics should be left alone. Basically, there are some songs that just shouldn't be done. 'Summertime Blues' shouldn't be done; I don't think the Who should have done it. 'Hound Dog', no one should ever record, or 'Heartbreak Hotel'. You just don't do it.

Sally: Are you still working with Nick Lowe at all, despite the split?

Dave: No, not for ages. He's been busy with Carlene, doing her next album. I suppose our paths will cross again.

MOTORHEAD

The lads arrived at their record company's H.Q. for our interview a little bit the worse for wear. They'd just fallen off the plane from Belfast after an exhausting trip and were counting the minutes till the boozers opened. However, we managed to have a very illuminating conversation and quite a few laughs although I did have to translate some of the language. I also carefully edited out Phil's vivid account of his experience with a catheter whilst in hospital – definitely not for the squeamish . . .

Sally: You've just come back from Belfast. What was it like over there?

Phil: Great, the audiences over there were fantastic. They're really glad when a band goes over there, because a lot of people are afraid to go; they think they're going to get shot at, be caught in crossfire, but it's all bullshit really. You're not gonna get shot or killed 'cause they're really glad you're over there.

Sally: Aren't you at all scared when you're over there?

Phil: I was in hospital when I did my neck and I got to know the nurses really well and they were great. I fancied a few of them and they said, 'Next time you come back you must come and see us.' The only time I had to go and see them was after the sound check and before the show, so I sneaked out of the gig and said hello. When we were coming out the guy who came to collect me said, 'Christ almighty, I don't know how we're going to get back to the gig; there's all that shooting going on'. We could hear the cracks of rifles going off and all the barriers were down and there were soldiers running about.

Sally: I know you have to plan a year ahead. What's on the cards for '82?

Lemmy: We're doing America this year. When we come back we're going to do a bit more of Europe and then an English tour in January then America again in February.

Phil: We've got two albums coming out this year; we've got the live one, then when we come back from the States we have to go into the studio to record a studio album.

Sally: How long do you spend in the studio when you do a studio album?

Lemmy: Five weeks, the last one.

Sally: Do you write as you go along, or do you write whilst you're on the road?

Lemmy: We usually go into the studio and spend a couple of weeks just getting tunes together – roughs – then I write them afterwards at the studio. I do all the words you see.

Phil: Lemmy's very good at it. I've occasionally submitted some lyrics that I've written but Lemmy absolutely refuses to sing them, so I don't try any more.

Sally: So you get the music together first?

Phil: Yes. We go down the studio and we jam. We always have a little cassette player to roughly record it and when you're playing together something clicks. You come up with a good riff so you stop and listen back to it and you end up with a tapeful of riffs and jams and you just keep playing them back and say, 'That bit might go; put this bit with that bit.' That's basically how a song comes together. Then Lemmy takes the tape away and whenever he's in the mood, he listens to the tune and dashes off a quick lyric.

Phil: On the last album we had four songs left that hadn't got any lyrics and me and Eddie said, 'Lemmy, you've really got to write these lyrics you know,' and he said, 'I wanna go to the * * ** boozer.' Eventually he said, 'Oh * * * *, all right, stop asking me. Leave me alone for half an hour.' Miraculously, he wrote the lyrics for four songs and they were all really good. We were amazed.

Sally: So where do you get this great inspiration to be able to work so quickly. Is it pressure, thinking, 'God, I've got to do it?'

Lemmy: No, no, it's not that at all 'cause I never feel I've got to do it. If I'm in the mood I just do it and it just comes dead easy.

Eddie: We thought we'd finished the last album. We got down the studio all happy then Vick turned round and said, 'You're ten minutes short, you've got to write another couple of tracks.' That's why they were such a rush.

Sally: What about your teaming up with Girlschool?

Phil: Well, we first met Girlschool when we signed to Bronze and were looking for a support band for the 'Overkill' tour. We were sent a single by a group called Girlschool and we listened to them and thought, 'Christ, this is pretty good really.' So Douglas said, 'Go and see the girls rehearsing and see if they can actually play as good as they sound.' Usually girl bands look much better than they play. Lemmy was the only one who went down and he came back and said, 'Really good.' We said, 'Right,' because if one of us is that positive about something we'll go for it.

Lemmy: We work very closely. We trust one another's judgement.

Phil: So we got them on the tour and we've been very good friends ever since.

Sally: Will you tour with them again?

Phil: We can't afford to do too many tours with them for either of our sakes.

Eddie: Maybe a Christmas record. I think that might be nice.

Lemmy: I think we'll probably stick a record out every year together – something like that.

Sally: It was 1975 wasn't it, Lemmy, when you got Motorhead together? It must seem a lifetime away now. What was your idea at that point?

Lemmy: The press release that I did at the time sums it up fairly well. I said I was going to form the nastiest band in the history of rock and roll and if we moved in next door to you your lawn would die.

Sally: Do you think you've achieved that?

Lemmy: Yeah, I think I've gone way over the achievement.

Sally: So how did Phil and Eddie get involved?

Lemmy: They had a car.

Sally: Big pull that!

Lemmy: Oh, yeah. We were doing this record in Rockfield and I said to Phil, 'You're a drummer, aren't you? If you'd like to come to Rockfield, bring your drums with you'. He said, 'Yes, yes.' It was him, me and Larry then and Larry was always groaning to get another guitarist. Phil and I both knew Eddie so we got him and Larry never came to another rehearsal!

Sally: And then there were three! Had you intended to have four of you but just never got around to having a fourth one?

Lemmy: Yeah. I wasn't going to be the singer, 'cause I'd never been the lead singer in a band. I was going to get another guitar player and a singer, but it just worked out that the three of us work very well together and we said, 'Well, this way we'll get more money.'

Sally: So at that stage you'd made a record.

Eddie: The record was made but they wouldn't release it.

Sally: Why wouldn't they release it?

Eddie: Too terrible, I suppose.

Phil: Let's clarify the situation. When Lemmy left Hawkwind, who were on United Artists, Lemmy said, 'I'm forming this band.' U.A. said they'd keep him on and pay for the recording costs, etc. When we'd finished it, me and Lemmy used to go down to U.A. at least twice a week to find out when it was coming out and they'd say, 'It's been delayed.' That went on for three or four months. Then they finally told us the truth – that basically they didn't think it was any good and they weren't going to release it.

Lemmy: Then they wouldn't release *us* either because we owed them for the recording costs.

Eddie: But eventually it did come out last year when we were becoming successful.

Sally: Did you mind that?

Phil: In a way, because Eddie wasn't on it, so it wasn't really representative of Motorhead now. For a start, it's very slow and ponderous. At the same time it was good because it helped to pay off the eighteen grand that we owed U.A. So it was good in one way and bad in another.

Sally: After your U.A. problems it took quite a while for things to happen, didn't it?

Lemmy: Yes, two years without anything.

Phil: We were labelled for a long time. Every time our name was mentioned in the press it was detrimental – 'The world's best, worst band in the world'. Nobody would touch us or even speak to us, and as regards record companies, they just said, 'Go away'.

Sally: Did you ever feel like breaking up, jacking the whole thing in during that time?

Phil: We nearly did.

Eddie: In April '77 we did the Marquee. We were gonna support the Damned and Phil and I said, 'We'll knock it on the head after the gig.' So we thought we'd get a mobile down just to get something of Motorhead on tape. Then Lemmy said, 'There's a guy at Chiswick who's been trying to get hold of us.' It wasn't possible to get a mobile, so he said, 'Go and make a single.'

Phil: This was Ted Carroll, by the way. After we'd been in the studio for two days, Ted came down from London to listen to the single; and without telling him we suddenly presented him with eleven tracks which we'd done in two days. He was amazed. He's great, Ted, he really is. He's a diamond.

Eddie: He saved Motorhead.

Phil: So for the cost of a single he had an album.

Lemmy: He put the album out and I think it's still the biggest selling record that Chiswick have ever made.

Sally: Last year was the year when it all really came together. Has it changed you much having success?

Lemmy: No. I still smell . . .

Eddie: We used to have drinks with audiences but we can't really do that any more 'cause they go mad.

Sally: Your whole fan following is incredibly strong, isn't it? That was even before you had record success.

Phil: That's what kept us going because we knew there were a lot of kids out there who loved us. We were doing small gigs and getting paid £150 and it was costing us £175 to do them. In the early hours of the morning we'd get back to London and you get a pound or something. Basically it was the kids who kept us going. I know it sounds a bit corny like, but it's true – if it wasn't for those kids we would have split up.

Sally: You had a bit of trouble with one particular fan, didn't you, when you had your accident at Christmas?

Phil: He was a friend really. We'd met him before in Belfast and we were drinking in the bar in the hotel till halfpast five and were drunk. By that time all the ladies had gone so there wasn't much point in hanging around. As we waited for the lift, we wanted to see who could lift each other the highest. This fan was a big bloke and I tried to lift him up, but I could hardly move him. Then he picked me up, lifted me above his head and, of course, he . . .

Lemmy: . . . fell backwards.

Phil: I fell – bang! – straight on my head. I didn't spill much of my drink though.

Sally: Very good, well trained.

Lemmy: And everybody else got up laughing and he was still on the floor. I was going, 'Come on Phil, stop messing about, get up.'

Phil: I stood up and just as I stood up I remember the lift doors opening and I was saying to Lemmy, 'Oh Christ, my neck hurts.'

Lemmy: And then he blacked out.

Phil: The next thing I remember is waking up in the hospital with people saying, 'You've got a broken neck.'

Sally: There were stories that you were going to be paralysed.

Phil: Lemmy and Mick came to the hospital with us and because it was so early in the morning there was only a trainee doctor on. The guy said, 'Well, we've X-rayed him and he's got three fractures in his neck. I'm not qualified to say how bad they are, but if it is bad he could be in hospital for anything up to four months and he could even be in traction.' So Lemmy and Mick left the hospital with these varying stories.

Sally: Did they tell you that you might not walk again?

Phil: Yes, they laid it on. I was quite worried.

Sally: Only quite worried!

Phil: Well, not that worried, because I could move my fingers and my toes; but in hospital they won't tell you anything until they're one hundred per cent sure. I was in hospital for five and a half days, and it wasn't until the fourth day that the actual top notch doctor came round and said, 'Well, Philip, I have got some good news for you. It's not as serious as we thought. They're only hairline fractures. You'll just have to have a collar on for a few days and you can go home the day after tomorrow.' It was more of an inconvenience, you know – a pain in the neck!

Sally: Oh, no! How many times have you said that?

Phil: How many times have I had it said to me! I've had all the neck jokes, but basically it was more of a hindrance than really serious. The only serious thing about it was that I was told I mustn't get drunk and I mustn't fall over because I had this collar on. Of course, you can't see your feet and for the first two days while I was in London, I went out to Dingwalls' and the Venue but I realised that they were telling me the truth. I couldn't see the ground, and you know in clubs it's dark and you never know exactly who's lying on the floor. Douglas, our Manager, said, 'Right, you're not staying in London over Christmas because there's parties to go to and you won't be able to resist.' I must say, after spending five and a half days in the New Road surgery ward and seeing all those poor unfortunate people, I realised how lucky I was. I went off to Leeds and stayed with my parents for almost three weeks. I just sat in front of the fire in front of the telly in the most comfortable chair and got pissed, but I was safe because my mum and dad wouldn't let me do anything. After about two weeks, you know, all I wanted to do was to take the rubbish out and one day they caught me and my mum went mad. She was shouting at my dad, 'Colin, he's moved! Philip, what do you think you're doing? You sit down. You bloody well stop that. You go and sit down!' I couldn't do anything.

Eddie: His mum and dad are great. They come to some of the gigs.

Phil: My mum's a headbanger. My dad says, 'You should've seen your mum the other day – she was up there bangin' away!'

Sally: Are they proud of you?

Phil: Of course they are. Well, at school I was a no-hoper. I was always being told by my family and teachers in school reports there was no chance. 'God knows what he's going to end up doing.' I am quite proud of myself. The only things I was any good at at school was gymnastics and woodwork.

Sally: Do you see yourselves Motorheadbanging in ten years' time?

Lemmy: I see us as a Status Quo sort of thing, just going on.

Sally: I know you are also quite interested in production and management.

Eddie: I produced the Girlschool's dance demos which got them a deal.

Lemmy: I would really like to get into the management side.

Sally: You wouldn't have the time at the moment, would you?

Lemmy: Not at the moment, but you can be a silent partner in a management team.

Eddie: Production is a thing we should get into, 'cause I think individually we're all very acute at sussing out the sounds.

Sally: Do you get upset that people don't give you credit for much intelligence?

Lemmy: It gets a bit boring after a while. You get a bit tired of being referred to as long-haired morons with leather jackets, but that's obviously our cross and we grin and bear it.

Phil: It's obvious to us that the sort of people who think that are probably more like morons than we are. We are what we are and I really hate people who sell out just to make money because when you do you actually change yourself from what you naturally want to do. Then obviously, it's not to do with the music, it's to do with making money. When we all started off our intention was never to become huge millionaires, we just enjoyed playing music, but the natural progression is, as you get more well known and your records sell, you start earning money.

Sally: What do you do with your money?

Phil: Spend it, spend it! We are still paying off a lot of debts that we incurred up until two years ago.

Lemmy: We buy toys and tape recorders.

Sally: Are there any bands that you particularly admire?

Eddie: The majority of the music we listen to is like Quo, ACDC, ZZ Top and all the old favourites, Zeppelin, Hendrix, Deep Purple.

Phil: Girlschool at the moment, and when I'm at home or on my own I really like reggae. That was the first music I was ever into.

Eddie: On the road it's usually Status Quo – 'Twelve Gold Bars'.

Sally: You spend a phenomenal amount of time together working. When you have actually got time off do you avoid each other like the plague?

Lemmy: No. At least twice a week we wind up in the same boozer – all on our hands and knees.

Phil: We have wonderful rows.

Sally: What about?

Phil: Who gets the last of the vodka. If, during a gig, one of us was playing out of time or if one of us cocked a number. But whatever happens, or however serious it gets, we make it up. Yeah, we've had a lot of fights . . . The classic quote was when Eddie and I were having a fight in a hotel in West Yorkshire. We were fighting about something in the bar during a drinking session after the gig and we were actually fighting under the table.

Lemmy: It was very funny actually. I was down the other end of the bar playing on the one-arm bandit and they were round the corner. All of a sudden, one of them came backwards with the other one after him. All these people scattered into the lift – they were fighting to get into the lift.

Phil: Somebody shouted, 'Get the tour manager' and he came down and he immediately grabbed hold of Eddie and was forcibly restraining him, so I started punching the tour manager.

Eddie: He made the classic quote.

Phil: 'If you can't punch your best friend in the mouth, who can you punch?' Once you're really firm friends, and you've been friends for a long time, and the arguments and the fights stop, then I think that's the beginning of the end of the friendship.

RICK PARFITT

Rick Parfitt appeared on 'Tiswas' on March 21st. Many of you will have seen him displaying his trim new figure as a flower in Compost Corner. Prior to his appearance I had rung his manager to ask if he would enact this role for us and was told that he didn't think it was at all Rick's cup of tea. However, when Rick arrived and I explained to him what we wanted him to do he was delighted and couldn't wait to get into the green leotard!

When the show finished Rick was supposed to go straight to the N.E.C. (National Exhibition Centre) for a sound check, but he kindly let me drag him off to the dressing room for a chat . . .

Sally: Rick, you are nearing the end of your first British tour for two years. Was there any special reason for staying off the road for so long?

Rick: Yes. We felt at the end of the last tour we wanted a break. We'd been working our balls off for the last eight years solid, so we decided to take a year off. About three or four months into that year everybody was getting really pissed off; it just wasn't like us not to be working. We planned the tour for a year later, but then I had a few problems with my legs. I got some sort of arthritis and I literally couldn't tour, so we had to cancel that and wait till all the halls were available and till I got better.

Sally: How did you cure the problem with the legs?

Rick: I went to Germany, because they are, I think, far more advanced than us. They wrapped me up in mud, and I thought, 'What is all this?' But it's a great cure. They wrap you up in hot mud and the natural earth draws all the badness out of your body with a few injections.

Sally: How long did that whole process take?

Rick: I was in hospital for just over two weeks.

Sally: It was an arthritic condition?

Rick: Yes – sero-negative polio-arthritis of the spine, which worried me sick. My joints were all stiffening up and I had visions of me sitting there all crippled up, but being the strong lad that I am I got over it, and I am OK now.

Sally: So that put you off for a year. What did everyone get up to during that time off?

Rick: Well, there was some recording going on, as I was able to record. I could still play, although I had bad hands and it was really difficult. We did quite a lot of writing. In fact, we did two albums. I'm just pleased it has all come together now and we're out on the road again, because after that length lay-off the thought of being on the road is almost frightening. At the first gig we were very nervous, very uptight, worrying if it was going to be all right, and as it happens the first gig wasn't. Obviously it wasn't going to be after all that time. The second gig was much better and it's just started to take shape now.

Sally: Do you have as much enthusiasm for it all now as when you started?

Rick: Yes, that's what surprises us. I couldn't believe it. Backtracking slightly, when we started out down in Cornwall, my God, the nerves and the wanting to go out and get that energy off – it's incredible. Also, because we're not using a support band we've increased the length of the set now.

Sally: You're always coming out with new material and I'm sure the fans that come want to hear that *and* all the oldies. How do you decide what you're going to put into the act?

Rick: It's very difficult. We pondered over this for ages.This was scrubbed, that was scrubbed, that was put in. We finally arrived at a set with all the oldies left in barring a couple. We kept all the old favourites and we've put six new songs in from the last two or three albums; even to put six songs in is really a big job. When you're established in what you are doing and you can do it with your eyes closed, to put six new songs in disrupts it; it creases that lovely smooth line. The only way to rehearse them is to get them on stage. The ones we know are nerve-racking enough, but then the new ones came along and you go, 'Oh, my God, am I going to remember the words?' But it went off all right.

Sally: It's also good to have the edge put into the act. If you were relying on all the old ones you've been doing for so long you could get complacent.

Rick: Yes, we really want to give the fans value for money, because it's not cheap to go and see a band nowadays and a lot of the fans don't earn that much dough. If someone wants to see the band and takes his girlfriend, it's going to cost twelve or thirteen quid. It's a lot of money, so we firmly believe, as we always have done, in giving value for money. We go out and work our balls off for two and a half hours.

Sally: How expensive is it for you to tour?

Rick: Immensely. You've obviously heard all this before, but it really is. There's no bullshit about that. You're talking about coaches for the band to travel in, hotel bills for thirty people – you don't want to stay in shit holes, so you stay in fairly decent hotels – food, drink, the trucking, the hiring of equipment . . . I'll be bluntly honest with you, we won't make a penny out of this. We've geared it, hopefully, that we won't lose, but we certainly ain't going to make any money.

Sally: You didn't tour with the 'Just Supposin' album, but it still sold very well, didn't it?

Rick: It did, yes. That's a thing that really surprised us, and we thought, 'It's amazing – we're not out on the road, we haven't done anything for ages and the album is still selling'. So we knew that the army was still out there and that's a really good thought. When we got back on stage, honestly, we were wondering about this, but the vibe is as good, if not better, than it was before.

Sally: Have any of you felt like going off and doing solo albums, as often happens with other bands?

Rick: The thought's in our heads, put it like that. I'm doing a bit of producing at the moment, producing a record my wife's doing.

Sally: What sort of music?

Rick: She's done a thing called 'Only Lonely' which is by J. D. Southern, but I want to write for her. We thought about doing solo projects, but there's so much going on with Quo that I just can't do it. At the moment I'm fully committed to Status Quo.

Sally: Have you ever talked of splitting up?

Rick: We've all said, 'That's it, I'm out.' Next day you wake up and think, 'What have I said?' you know, when the drink's worn off. No, I think there's plenty of life left in the band. It's proved it to me now. When we go on stage the energy is still there.

Sally: What about writing – how does that work?

Rick: Most of the writing occurs on the road, actually. When we're touring, we get back to the hotel at night and just sit around with a guitar, and something will happen, you get an idea. Most of the songs for the next album, which aren't written yet, not even thought of yet, will occur during the European tour. When we come back we should have an album.

Sally: Have you got 1982 planned?

Rick: Beware the Big Q in 1982, twenty years that is.

Sally: So will it be something special?

Rick: We haven't thought of anything outrageous yet. I figure there'll be a couple of parties.

Sally: And some special shows maybe?

Rick: Maybe. I'd like to think so but I don't know.

Sally: How did you get into shape this year? You'd been quite unfit, hadn't you?

Rick: I was nearly thirteen stone and I felt dreadful. It was terrible and a two-month tour was looming up. I thought, 'Christ, no way Parfitt, can you go out on stage like this.' I had no neck, I had no chin. I was just a big guff. Really, it was terrible, so I went to Harley Street. I didn't want to but I realised that I had to. I saw this very good doctor who certainly wasn't a quack – you can get quacks for losing weight; they give you all the uppers in the world and you steam around like a blue-arsed fly all day – but this guy was great. We sussed out that I had two months to do it in, and I stayed on this diet for six weeks and I lost two stone.

Sally: Knock out the booze?

Rick: Yes, I had to knock out the booze, butter, sugar, vegetables, salads, everything. Even a salad contains water, so I used to find myself eating a piece of steak on its own, or a piece of fish with freshly squeezed orange juice. That was it and I stuck to it. Willpower came, as I knew I had to go on tour. You know, it's the worst feeling in the world if you walk out on stage and you don't feel good. It's the worst. I kept that in the back of my mind and I think that's what did it for me – I made it. I'm ten and a half stone now, which is just about the right weight for me.

Sally: Presumably you are all financially set up forever really.

Rick: I'm skint.

Sally: How can you be skint?

Rick: Well, we won't go into it. We're all right, we're doing all right. I mean, at the moment I've got a nice house and a nice Porsche, the love of my life, apart from my wife – isn't that corny? But yes, we are doing all right, but I want to come out relaxed financially.

Sally: What sort of music do you listen to at home?

Rick: All sorts really. I got into quite a lot of new stuff recently, mainly because Marietta gets into it.

Sally: Anyone you particularly rate at the moment?

Rick: I used to like Squeeze very much. I listen to Robert Palmer. In the early days I really liked Cliff, and the Shadows had a big influence on me. I was a great Cliff fan. Funnily enough something happened to me very recently which I was really knocked out about. Cliff did some backing on Marietta's record and I sang along. Cliff comes up to the house from time to time and that to me is a milestone in my life – somebody who really, if you like, started me off playing a guitar. To actually think Cliff was coming to dinner totally did me up.

Sally: Are there any special ambitions in the band? You've cracked so many things, is there one outstanding thing you all really want to achieve?

Rick: I suppose to be the biggest band in the world. We're about number ten now.

Sally: Do you think there's any reason why you've kept going for so long, and you've kept being successful?

Rick: We like doing it. I look at it sometimes and see the trends that have come and gone, and I look at Quo as a kind of steam train that just buffets its way through all these trends and comes out the other side and is still shunting, you know, the fire is still alight. We don't conform to any trend of dress or music. We just play what we want and what we like so you'd best ask the fans because they keep digging it and they keep buying it, and we enjoy doing it. We've got a formula that works and we've been knocked something wicked for what we do. The people who don't really listen to it say it's all the same but, of course, it's not all the same. A lot of bloody hard work goes into what we do. As long as we've still got the enthusiasm there, we'll keep going.

SPANDAU BALLET

The band were happily relaxing in their record company's press office awaiting my arrival. They dress up in all those marvellous clothes even to record a taped interview! Before our conversation they proudly showed me their new video of 'Muscle Bound'.

Tony: I think British TV programmes are quite antiquated in their opinions of videos because nearly all groups do videos and some of them are exceptionally good. It seems to me 'Top of the Pops' has a limit of three videos per show, yet we're entering a video age – people are actually making good quality films. The days of a band just going on and playing in front of a cheap backdrop have gone now.

Steve: The first time we did 'Top of the Pops' they hadn't bothered to take any notice of what we wanted – you know, same old lights, etc.

Martin: 'Top of the Pops' is completely false. I remember the first time we did it . . . I mean, we'd all been watching 'Top of the Pops' for years since we were kids and we'd got this image of what it was going to be like.

Sally: You think it's going to have this tremendous atmosphere, don't you?

Martin: Yeah, but the stages are pretty small and then, the kids come in and they herd them in one corner and try to make it look like there's fifty people and then they sling a couple of records on and say, 'Right, enjoy yourselves, dance', and they have this woman who screams at them to have fun.

Tony: It's just a shame that 'Top of the Pops' is the only show at the moment, but it does serve a purpose.

Sally: Let's go back to the beginning for your life history.

Tony: Well, we left school and most of us just drifted into pretty boring jobs but we were always into looking good and being stylish.

Sally: Even when you were at school?

Tony: Yes, because we grew up around the seventies soul scene so we were going around clubs, dressing up, chatting up the girls and trying to impress them. We were dancing to good music and having a drink, so we sort of grew up through the scene and as time went on that became very much like the punk scene, manipulated by various sharks – it became a production line system. There were various small clubs, Billy's was the first one (it opened in 1978) that catered for something different; there was new music being played and there were lots of people really getting into that. Most kids were from the soul scene anyway or from the early punk scene. There were lots of people who were being really innovative – young journalists, sculptors, designers. Everyone was trying to contribute something and, if they weren't doing that, because a lot of them were just ordinary kids, then they contributed in looking good.

Martin: Yeah, everyone was really into something. They all had complete confidence but all you could hear over the Tannoy was music by old people like David Bowie, Bryan Ferry and stuff like that. People so much older than us, and there wasn't a group that you could turn around and say, 'That's our music'.

Tony: Yes, and it seemed a natural thing to form a group to fill that gap. There was no one there out of the ordinary. Everybody else was doing other things and we thought it was about time that we should reflect the new musical attitude. That's one reason why we differ so much from the majority of groups, because we evolved from the club scene rather than adopted an image.

Sally: After four months' rehearsal you invited fifty hypercritical people down to a reheasal studio in the Holloway Road. They were very impressed and if they hadn't been, I gather Spandau Ballet wouldn't exist today.

Tony: That's right.

John: From that we played Blitz and a couple of Christmas parties. But from the management point of view we had nothing signed until last October. We had a lot of interest but . . .

Tony: I think it was the first party we played a whole set: on the third song Chris Blackwell from Island Records said, 'THIS IS GREAT, THIS IS GREAT! I want to sign them, I want to talk business.' We went and talked business and it was quite a good deal but we felt that we had a long way to go. We didn't feel ready to sign because we knew that we could get a better deal; so we waited until we had every major record company in London after us. We literally played them off one against the other.

Martin: We always do everything in the best way possible – it stems from the fact that if we go out we never go out under-dressed. If I can't get dressed properly I won't go out, I stay in.

Sally: You've done hardly any gigs, have you?

Steve: The way we promote our records is not to do gigs but to do well-produced 12″ singles at discotheques and clubs. That's our form of promotion. We would rather do that than tour the country and do one-nighters.

Sally: You haven't advertised the gigs that you've done, have you?

Tony: There's been no need to advertise, let's be honest. Every show we've done, if we'd advertised them we would have upset too many – I mean enough people get upset now because they can't get in.

Steve: We were always very conscious of getting the wrong people to our gigs. I mean we could have a bunch of skinheads for example, who don't like us – don't like the 'poofs' walking around dressing up. There could be trouble, so that's one reason we don't advertise. The people we really want to come, the people that matter, the people that look good, who want to go out and enjoy themselves and come and see us, they know about it anyway . . . they'd be in the right places.

Sally: This is the ideal – to play where you want to play and that's perfectly understandable, but you're going to have pressure put on, because of the hit records you're having, to do bigger gigs.

Tony: We understand that. When we started off, we didn't see ourselves as a touring band, we weren't brought up in that environment. We thought of ourselves as making good records for clubs that people could dance to. Now we understand that there is a need, that kids do want to see us; they always want to see their idols, but just going back to the venues . . . I don't want to play the Music Machine. People get killed at the Music Machine, so that's not my scene. It's not a place that our audience would want to go to, it's not a place that I would want them to go to. There's beer stains all over the place. When we do choose a venue we choose a venue that we feel would be adequate for us, that would be a nice place to play in.

Sally: But these are going to be small places, aren't they?

Tony: Not necessarily, no. Some hold 1,500 people. We're now working on some sort of tour. We're just going to be playing a few dates around the country, probably about ten or eleven dates at the very most, at venues which we feel are suitable for us that will create a good atmosphere for our audience. I mean, why have a venue where an audience hears a bit of background music, sees the band, has a drink and goes home? Why not make it a five hour thing? I mean at the Sundown there were kids dancing three hours before we came on. We had music on, we had videos and old film shows, screens at the back with a sort of atmosphere and the audience created that.

Sally: Do you see this as a thing of the future, that maybe other bands will get into?

Tony: I think it's happening. They're going to have to.

Sally: Do you find that fashion designers latch on to you?

Tony: You get a lot of that. They say, 'I can make you something.' Now we've got more money, of course, we can look around and find more expensive clothes. There was a period when we didn't have that much money, but you can still make yourself look good. I mean, it's just a question of looking round second-hand shops and jumble sales. It's really a question of mixing and matching, it's an inbuilt kind of flair, it's an inbuilt style you've either got or you haven't got.

Martin: You can't buy it, you can't buy style.

Sally: You said earlier how much you enjoy making the video and you're also involved in designing your album covers. You seem to have your finger in everything.

Tony: When we signed up to Chrysalis we said we wanted artistic control. Record companies say, 'No problem, no problem', and you'll get it verbally but you won't get it written into the contract. We also wanted our own label, which we got, called Reformation. That's something we felt we could channel new ideas through and sign other acts to. We might be going for films. We're going to form our own publishing company.

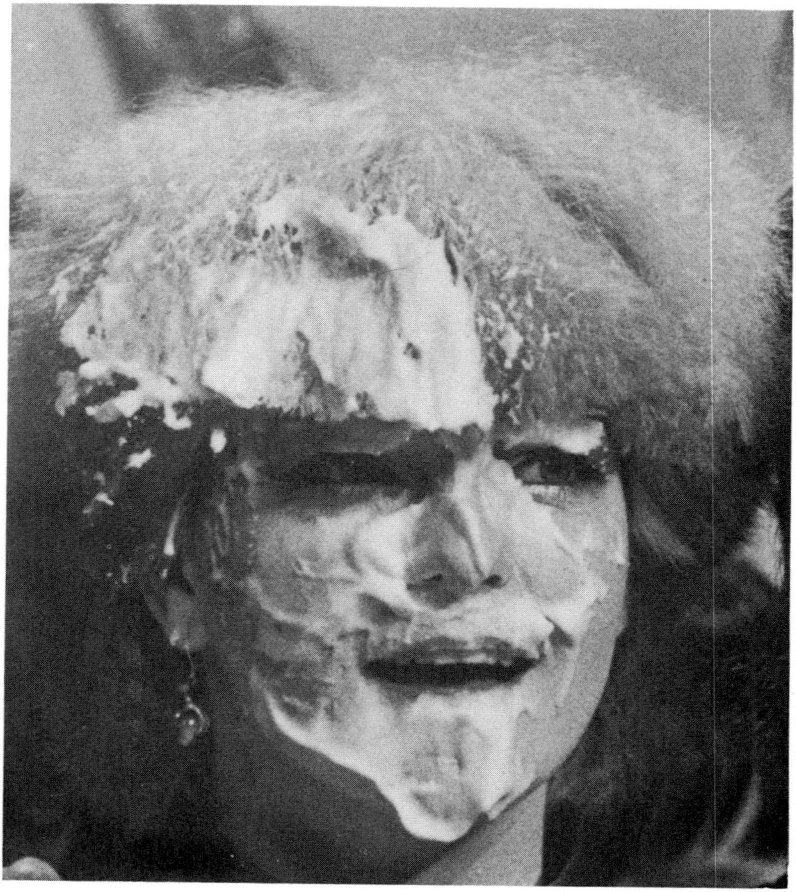

TOYAH

When Toyah appeared on 'Tiswas' she asked me to give her a custard pie on behalf of her Dad! Anything to oblige (see picture). It was such a pity though to ruin all the wonderful make-up she'd spent hours doing. But having ruined her face, we soon wrecked her hair as well by getting her to perform the Bucket of Water Supporters' Club song.

I managed to catch up with Toyah again on April 6th at the Marquee Studios in London.

Sally: You're in the studio now, working on your fourth album . . .

Toyah: We're bang in the middle. I was making 'Tales of the Unexpected' when the band started on the album. They went in and put a few tunes down and sent me the tape and I've written the lyrics to them. So it's been a very disjointed album up to now.

Sally: That's not normally how you work, is it?

Toyah: We usually write the songs beforehand, but instead we've gone straight in and written and I must say I never felt like this before. 'Blue Meaning' I was disappointed with, but I think this is the best music we have ever come up with.

Sally: How old were you when you first decided that you were going to be an entertainer?

Toyah: I was about nine. I wanted to be everything from a female S.A.S. agent to a nun, and then suddenly I got into ice-skating as a hobby, and that turned into about eight hours' training a day and I was going to become an ice skater. Then I went through a series of operations to straighten my toes out which went wrong. I was told I shouldn't skate because my toes would bend again, so I was made to stop skating. I just thought 'What the heck, I'll become a dancer', and I started to study dance very seriously, and then I really fell in love with the thought of acting and singing. It's a thing I've always wanted to do but never thought could happen to me because whenever I said I wanted to be an actress and singer, people just laughed and said, 'Yes, dear, you'll soon grow out of that.' It was people saying that that made me more determined to do it. I think if people hadn't laughed at me I wouldn't have done it.

Sally: How did you go about starting to do it?

Toyah: Well, my parents said I could do whatever I wanted but they would never help me. That's fair enough. They wanted me to be an artist because I was quite good at drawing, and I said, 'OK, right. Up yours'. I went and signed on at the local drama school, which was the Birmingham theatre, and I went there every weekend while I was still at school.

Sally: How did you manage to pay for that?

Toyah: I used to work in the evenings, in the wardrobe departments of the Alexandra Theatre and the Hippodrome, and then I went full time for a year after I left school. I averaged four hours sleep a night for a whole year. I was on about £2 a night for working wardrobe at the Alexandra Theatre and I had to get a hundred quid to pay the term's fee, so I was also working in a café in the Dolce Vita dance club, and at the wardrobe department at the Alex every night and weekends. I loved every minute. I was developing as my true self. My hair became how it is now. I got the clothes I wanted to wear and I no longer had to wear a uniform. I think it was the most fabulous time in my life. It was wonderful. I had no boyfriends, and there was everyone else having boyfriends, and getting into arguments and not being allowed out and I was the only free person in the whole school. People used to sort of hate me for it because I looked original, whereas everyone at drama school was saying, 'You can't act if you've got such a distinct image, no one will want you. You'll get typecast.'

Sally: When did you first become interested in music?

Toyah: My main ambition – to sing – happened as soon as Marc Bolan appeared in my life. I just thought he was wonderful, the glitter of him and his image. I remember 'Ride a White Swan' was the one that really got me into it. And then I went out and bought all the Tyrannosaurus Rex albums. I wasn't just in love with him; I was in love with what he was doing – I just wanted to do it. Then Bowie came along, and he was even bigger. I wanted to be that sort of personality. I remember seeing Bowie live, and I haven't recovered from it yet. I actually got hysterical. I was crying. I just couldn't believe it.

Sally: You've managed to combine being an actress and a singer, which is very difficult, as people don't usually get accepted on two levels.

Toyah: I don't think I am accepted. Let's go from the critics' point of view. The acting critics love me and the music critics hate me because they think I'm an actress cashing in on singing. But I don't give a damn about the music critics because I think they're the lowest of the low. To me, criticism is something that helps you; it says, 'Do this and it will make you better', but all the criticism I get is, 'Oh, she's a stupid old bitch', and that's just personal, silly gossip. So I've just ploughed ahead doing what I'm happiest doing. I don't need to run off on holiday all the time and I'm prepared to work a good twenty hour day sometimes. I think that's why it works.

Sally: How do you map out a year? Presumably you have to plan quite far ahead?

Toyah: Yes. What happens is that I plan the music, and when I've got a week or so off I phone the agent and say, 'Is there any work?' and she says, 'Yes, do you want this or do you want that?' and I pick.

Sally: You might be missing out on some really good acting roles by planning around the music.

Toyah: I could be, but she doesn't tell me about it.

Sally: So the music comes first?

Toyah: At the moment, because I have a hit single. But if an exceptional film came up and I've got the lead part, then the music has to wait. I have an excellent manager and an excellent agent, and they combine things, without bothering me over it because they both know what I want.

There's a lot of ideas I've got for live shows but I would need to earn a lot of money to do it. It's a vicious circle; I have to come up with some commercial items, but up to now my acting has financed all my ideas with the band. I do want to act in America because they're the people that have got the money to produce the best films. England is producing some very good films, but the trouble is that they fall down because of dialects. Cockney films are so popular in England at the moment, but in America, they flop because no one can understand the Cockney language. One of my ambitions is either to do a great big sci-fi or horror movie – something I'd really like to see myself. I'm working on that at the moment.

Sally: You seem to have tremendous energy.

Toyah: I think my greatest asset is that I can turn off. A lot of people say, 'Why aren't you talking?' or 'What's the matter?' but I'll be completely turned off. To me it's a form of transcendental meditation: you can gain as much in twenty minutes as you can in eight hours' sleep.

Sally: I read somewhere that you don't have holidays and you don't have friends because you are so totally immersed in your career. Is that true?

Toyah: It's true about friends. I just have so little time. Really my career is all I want to live for. I don't want it to sound as dramatic as that, but that's all I want. I don't enjoy parties, I don't enjoy nightclubs, I don't enjoy wine bars, the social things. The only thing I do enjoy is cinema. I think the magic of cinema is amazing. It's one thing I would like to keep alive. If I could have a say in it I'd love to keep the cinemas of Britain and get the prices down so people could go every night.

Sally: Do you think it's harder for women to make it in this business?

Toyah: I think it's bitchier, definitely bitchier. It's well known that women have more weaknesses than men and if you knock them enough you can make them break. I think a lot of male critics try to attack us because we've probably got where they wanted to get. But I don't mind. I don't think like a woman. I've been writing this album and I realise every song I sing is as though a man's singing it. I've written it as though I'm a man. I do quite often forget I'm female. I just think I'm a living object, not male or female.

Sally: You're getting married soon, aren't you?

Toyah: Yes, it's a bit funny. It's supposed to be a secret. I'm keeping it a secret because everyone I know is trying to stop me from doing it.

Sally: Are they? Why?

Toyah: They just think the fans won't like me any more, which is understandable, but I think if we do it tastefully enough and quietly enough, the fans won't have to worry about it.

Sally: Do children come into your line of vision at all?

Toyah: No, no way. I haven't got the courage to have a child. I really haven't. I've seen what women have to go through and I know I haven't got the courage to do that. That's one respect I have for a married housewife – I couldn't go through what they go through. I'd be terrified.

Sally: Your looks have changed quite a lot over the years.

Toyah: Yes, I get bored with myself. I look in the mirror and I don't like what I see, so I go out and change it. I'll never go so far as having plastic surgery or anything like that though. But I have a hair change every week. I've got this collection of colours at home and I just slap something on for no other reason than my own taste. The same goes for clothes. I've got this one designer and I just think her clothes are fabulous. I wear them all the time. I think she happens to be quite outrageous and very futuristic. I'd rather keep ahead or try to create my own fashion than copy someone else.

Sally: You've lost a lot of weight over the last two years. How did you do it?

Toyah: It was pure starvation – with a little help from certain drugs. It was the only way I could do it. I was twenty, I'd never had a boy friend and I was a very lonely person. I thought, 'Right, I am not going to eat', and I stopped eating for about two weeks. I lost a stone, then I started to eat sensibly, lost another stone and then another half stone. I was about 10½ stone.

Sally: How do you keep it down now?

Toyah: It's the touring that does it. We do so much touring that I get very little time to eat properly, so it just stays down. I've put on about a stone within the last year and I'm going to a health farm in the next two weeks to get it off – but I will never get as fat as I was, because it was horrible, horrible.

Sally: Have you changed much in the last couple of years, apart from your looks?

Toyah: I'm not as naïve as I used to be. God, I was thick when I was eighteen.

Sally: How much do you get involved in the production of your records?

Toyah: Totally. I'm here the whole time. But Nick Tauber, our producer, is very good – he knows what I mean when no one else knows what I'm going on about. I say, 'I want this, want that, you've got to do it', and he can understand me.

Sally: Is there anything looking back that you're really proud of?

Toyah: I am never one hundred per cent happy with what I do. I'm proud that I haven't cracked up yet.

Sally: Well, that's being able to switch off, I'm sure.

Toyah: And I am proud that I haven't let my enemies pull me down. If there are any budding young singers out there who read this, never, never let the critics hurt you because that's what they want. I'm positive. That's why I am so anti certain music critics, because they're so hurtful.

Sally: So do you actually read the critics?

Toyah: Doing this album I won't have a music paper near me because it does hurt me. I really do get hurt – thank God – because it shows I've got some sensitivity in me still. I read all my live reviews because that's where I want guidance, but you don't always get it. You just get these horrible personal things again.

Sally: You said that you're toughened up and that you used to be very naïve. So you see yourself as a very hard person?

Toyah: I'm not hard at all; I just cover it up. I'm sure sometimes I look as tough as hell, but I'm having a good cry inside.

Sally: I think that's the hardest thing about being a woman, in this business. You've got to be so tough all the time, even if you're not feeling it.

Toyah: Yes, you mustn't show weak links. To a man weakness means 'He's not trained in that area'. To a woman it means you have no hope. You've got to be better than men to be accepted by men. Even then you're only accepted on a lower level.

ULTRAVOX

Ultravox were rehearsing when I caught up with them. I'd met Midge many years before when he was in the teenybop band Slik and they'd appeared on a Saturday morning show I used to present called 'Saturday Scene'. It was interesting to see him again and talk about his, and indeed Ultravox's, long slow climb to success . . .

Sally: When did Ultravox originally form?

Warren: April 1974.

Sally: You, Billy and Chris were in the original line-up. It took a long time for anything to happen, didn't it, even though a lot of people knew about you?

Chris: It was a period when you had to be a working band. We managed to build up a real strong following but that's as far as it got because at that point we were record companyless and managementless. It's the same old story really.

Sally: But you did release records eventually.

Chris: Oh yeah, through Island, but that went drastically wrong and we just had to change everything which we managed to do eventually.

Sally: Were you playing the same sort of music then as you are now?

Chris: Yeah, basically.

Sally: Did you consider jacking it in when John Foxx left a couple of years ago?

Billy: Well, I think when that happened we all decided that we were going to continue, but for about three or four months things looked probably the grimmest.

Warren: That was just an amalgamation of all kinds of things. Like Chris said, we had no record company, no money, no manager, no nothing. We had no guitarist and no singer. It was just the three of us.

Billy: That whole thing happened in San Francisco at the end of a fairly hectic tour so when we came back we were a bit depressed. We got kicked off the label and we were stuck for money. Then we went in to rehearse more or less straight away, which was good because we kept going. Then we did the tour, and then we broke up at the end. It did take us a while for everything to sink in.

Warren: That's when Billy met up with Midge.

Midge: We met at Billy's which was the forerunner of the Blitz Club. I was toying with the idea of working with our favourite musicians Visage, and Billy was one of them. When I first met him they were just going to tour America. I didn't know about the split and it wasn't until they came back and said that John and Robin had left (Billy and I had done some work in the studio as Visage) that the light hit me and I thought, 'Ultravox – we're destined, we're made for each other!' At that point, as we said earlier, we had all kinds of problems. I had management of my own but no record company because they were suing me. Between us we owed the world millions!

Sally: Why were you being sued?

Midge: The Rich Kids broke up and we owed them four albums. They wanted the money so they had to get it from somebody.

Billy: We had those kinds of problems as well. Things looked pretty impossible. Because Island were asking for the next record company that signed us to pay them.

Sally: To get their recording costs back . . .

Midge: Which is only natural, but it was a bad situation for the four of us getting together.

Sally: And all being in the same state!

Midge: Yeah, it was ridiculous. We went straight into rehearsals to see if the idea would work. It felt good so we wrote a couple of songs in a couple of days and then we parted for six months because we had to keep it very quiet that we were together. Billy went off and did some work with Gary Numan and Warren worked with Zaine Griff. Chris did some photography and I went off and did some work with Thin Lizzy. It was all to make money to put into Ultravox.

Sally: Did you all end up paying off your record companies or are they still hammering on your doors?

Midge: We kept it really quiet what we were doing and we managed to body swerve it a wee bit. We came to agreements with the record companies whereby they wouldn't hound us for the rest of our lives.

Sally: Now, Midge, you had a fairly tough time after the Slik break-up. After that screaming adoration from the teenybop fans was it difficult for you to cope with life again?

Midge: The hardest bit was the come down from it all. One minute you were way up there and the next minute nobody wanted to know. That was the hardest part to cope with but I think if you can get through that you can through just about anything. Financial problems and things you just take as they come.

Sally: Didn't you make money out of that period?

Midge: No, I lost a fortune. I owed Slik money as well. I've owed everybody money. It made a lot of money for some people but it didn't make it for Slik or the management. We never saw any.

Sally: Has it made you more aware this time round?

Midge: Oh, yes. You learn a lot; it's an expensive lesson but I'll never do it again. I'll never make the same mistake.

Chris: The 'Midge Ure Business Course'!

Midge: Yes, 'Young Businessman of the Year'!

Sally: This is the difficult thing about this business, isn't it? Unless you've got some sort of business acumen you can really get ripped off through not understanding the pitfalls.

Chris: Yeah. When you're young and someone offers you £5,000 advance you think, 'Great, we'll do a single for £5,000.' You don't realise you're signing yourself away.

Midge: If a record sells millions like 'Forever and Ever' did, someone's making a hell of a lot of money and it's not you. You've signed a bit of paper saying you'll take tuppence for your work.

Sally: Yes, exactly. How did you pick yourself up after that tremendous success and get yourself going again?

Midge: I moved to London for a start. During the Slik thing I'd stayed in Scotland. I moved to London to join the Rich Kids – a fresh start for me, breaking away from what I'd done before. I tried that for a year and a half to two years but it just didn't work out. We did the one album. The musical differences were just too great.

Sally: Let's go back two years to when you all got together. You hadn't got a deal, you hadn't got management, you hadn't really got anything. Then you went over to America . . .

Midge: Yes. We got a loan from the Nat West. We'd actually met up with our management before we went to the bank, but they weren't managing us at the time. They were looking after us because they looked after Thin Lizzy. I'd been in contact with them so they handled things for us, helping us out a bit with the loan from the bank. We packed all the equipment as excess baggage and jumped on a Laker fight and bang – we were in America. We did a six-week tour.

Sally: You went there to break the act in?

Warren: It was much easier for us to do it in America, because if we toured in England, no matter how many people came to see the shows, we were bound to lose money because we had to supply a P.A. system, lights and all that sort of thing. You don't need to do that in America. We could tour in clubs and not have to cart all that around. It was actually financially better.

Sally: They've got it better set up over there, have they?

Chris: Yeah, they've got lots of places like that and it doesn't cost you so much money. The other reason we didn't want to do a tour of England at the time was because it was far too soon and it would have put us on the spot – we would have been under a microscope.

Sally: It might be cheaper to go and do it in America but were you still sufficiently well known over there to get people to come and see you?

Billy: Yes. We still attracted a lot of people even though they knew the band had virtually split up.

Sally: So when you came back, how did you go about trying to break into records, management and all that merry-go-round?

Midge: We had great ideas when we went to America, thinking we'd like to sign to an American record company and try it from that end. I'd failed from here – Ultravox had failed from here – so we thought we'd try it from a different angle. We had a couple of very interested record companies who came to see us and watched us rehearse. We were writing 'Vienna' at the time. We refused to do demos, we hate it; so they came in and heard us writing 'Vienna' and this bloke asked us if we could run through some of the set. We said,

'No, we can't because we're writing a piece of music and we don't want to get away from it'. So he sat and listened to the song '- he must have heard it about fourteen times that day – and then he went away and decided he didn't want to sign us! So what we did was set up a gig in London 'cause we hadn't done anything there with the new format and Chrysalis saw us.

Sally: So you got a deal pretty quickly once you came back?

Midge: Oh yeah, it didn't take long at all. The strange thing was, nobody heard anything. One guy from the record company had heard us live, he hadn't heard any other material. So they said, 'Go in the studio and do what you want. Don't do demos, just do anything.' We recorded 'Sleepwalk' which was our first single. We also recorded most of the album before we signed the deal. We recorded it within a couple of weeks then went out to Germany for ten days to mix it.

Sally: Do the four of you write together?

Warren: Yeah.

Sally: Presumably in the old line-up you used to write together as well. Have you noticed a big change now you've got Midge?

Warren: It's a lot more democratic.

Sally: Are you managing to make money now?

Warren: Any money that we've seen, whether it's been advances or whatever, it's all gone back into our equipment.

Billy: It's so expensive because you've always got to keep updating everything.

Sally: But you might be into profit soon.

Warren: Yes, we might. I think the fact that it's taken all of us so long, working really hard with no real returns other than a cult following, helps keep our feet on the ground.

Sally: Have you got a long term plan?

Midge: Just to keep coming up with something that we find interesting, because I think if *we* find it interesting, someone else will. You can't tailor what you're doing to suit a particular audience. We've just done a new album and on that album there isn't another 'Vienna' 'cause we deliberately didn't want to do that. We did that two years ago but everyone expects us to come out with a new 'Vienna'. We won't do it. We've just got to keep two steps ahead.

Warren: That's one of the reasons why it's taken us a long time to achieve success, because we've kept changing our music. If we'd kept making similar albums, we would have been successful a lot sooner because it takes people time to get to know you and get into your music. They like one album so then they get your next album and so on. It's a more durable kind of success when you do it our way. It doesn't come as quickly, but when you get it, it lasts.

Sally: Who's idea was it to make the promotion film for 'Vienna' such an epic?

Midge: Ours. The song lends itself to that. It's a new area that we've found ourselves getting involved in quite heavily.

Warren: The whole business of doing videos where the band is playing in a room or out in a field is such a hackneyed approach. We all really like movies so it's an ideal opportunity to make our own.

Sally: So you created how that should be. But something like that costs a fortune.

Chris: It didn't actually – it was very reasonable, about £15,000.

Sally: That's a lot of money.

Chris: It's got loads of showings, especially on cable TV in America.

Warren: Our first film, 'Passing Strangers' got runner-up award for best video of 1980.

Sally: I was talking to Spandau Ballet the other day who are with your record company and who made a good 'epic' video for 'Muscle Bound'. It seems Chrysalis are into spending money on videos.

Midge: Since 'Vienna' they are. We fronted the money for that. We did that ourselves to convince them that it was the right thing to do.

Sally: Did you get your money back?

Midge: Yeah, as soon as they saw the video.

KIM WILDE

Kim Wilde was a very difficult lady to track down as she's been out of the country a lot promoting 'Kids in America'. However, we finally got together in RAK Records office and, while she munched her way through egg rolls and grapefruit (she eats constantly and never puts on any weight – how I hate her!), we had a chat . . .

Sally: Your life must have changed quite dramatically over the last three months.

Kim: I'm a lot busier. The last month or two I've been making the album so I've spent most of my time in the studio.

Sally: You started making the album immediately after the single was released, did you?

Kim: Well, we'd always intended making an album, even before 'Kids in America' was a hit. Ricky was writing so much it seemed sacrilege not to put it down. I've also been doing a lot of things abroad as well. It's quite amusing how other countries go about interpreting your songs through their cameras. It's completely different from how they might do it here. Their music scene isn't too bright though.

Sally: They still look to England, don't they? Which place, apart from Britain, do you think has the best TV?

Kim: I think Germany is really good. All of their programmes knock spots off ours in many respects. Their pop programmes are great, although they only have them once a month, or a special every six weeks and in that kind of situation they can obviously afford to go to town and plan it a long time ahead. Musik Laaden in Germany was fantastic; one minute you were looking at Sister Sledge and the next minute a clip of Sonny and Cher doing 'I Got You Babe'.

Sally: Do you find that you can still walk down the street?

Kim: I can still walk down the street, but I don't get a kick out of doing things like that anymore. I used to like moseying around and buying things but now it's, get the car as close to the shop as possible, get in, know what you are going to get, get it, then home. There's no sort of happy browsing anymore, especially where I live, but in London it's different because there are so many people. I don't think they look at each other so much.

Sally: No, they don't, and there are so many stars floating around that I don't think they take much notice. London's about the best place to be.

Kim: It is in a way. I don't mind people taking double looks sometimes, but where I live it's a bit dodgy. I don't like shopping around there very much. They don't really bother me, but the trouble is I get too sensitive and if someone says something not very nice I get really upset about it.

There's an attitude among the public that buy the records – they think they own you. Like you owe them something. Gary Numan summed it up really well in an interview the other day. He said, 'I don't owe them anything. I was just there and I gave them music and they liked it and they don't owe me anything either.' It's not a callous attitude, it's just a very real one, that's what I feel. It's not that I feel malicious towards them. It's just that you like to have your privacy.

Sally: You've certainly captured the imagination of the press, haven't you? I think you've had coverage in practically every paper and magazine. They've all homed in on the same story, haven't they?

Kim: Of me and Dad and Rick, yeah.

Sally: Have you got fed up with that?

Kim: Well, I think I would have got fed up with it had Dad not been such an important part of my career; if he'd just been a rock and roll star of the fifties. The fact is he co-writes and is very helpful in the studio and I couldn't be without him. He's a great help and great friend. For that reason I don't mind, but I do get annoyed sometimes and say, 'Look, I can't stand any more questions about my dad. Go and ask him yourself.' They shut up then, but basically the press are out to do their job like anybody else so I don't mind co-operating.

Sally: Your dad must have helped you to keep your feet on the ground when it all went mad for you. It would have been quite hard to cope with that sudden success if you had no one around who understood the business.

Kim: My mother helped as well. I think the family were great to me. I never felt like my feet were ever going to leave, even when the record was going up the charts. It's given me a hell of a lot more confidence, but as for my feet leaving the ground, I don't think they ever will; they haven't yet, anyway. I suppose it's the way I've been brought up. I mean, my dad has never been one to mix socially with people in the business, not because they aren't nice but because that's the way he is. I haven't been brought up with stars at my doorstep and also with Dad being on the road for a long time now, you just see that it's a job like anything else.

Sally: I gather even when you were at art school you were hoping to get into music?

Kim: Yes. I did an 'A' Level in art at school. Everyone gets scared when it's time to leave school. They either decide to go out in the big world or sort of carry on being looked after by the system. I got into art and, luckily, it came along at a really great time. I got into college at St. Albans, but even then I was hoping I could get a singing career going alongside it. There was never any doubt which choice I would make if the opportunity arose.

Sally: Had you ever tried to start a singing career?

Kim: For a long time I'd been in the studios; they were like second homes to me. My mum's a backing singer; she used to take lower harmony, I'd take the higher harmony. We used to work with Dad on stage in the old days.

Sally: How old were you?

Kim: About sixteen. We used to tour up and down the country doing 'oo bops' and 'doo wahs'. We had fun doing that. Even before then, when I was eleven, I used to do all the vocal backings on Ricky's earlier hits and I always let it be known that I wanted to sing. I think everyone that really knows me has known that for a long time; it's not a sudden thing.

Sally: So the opportunity arose when Ricky wrote the song?

Kim: The opportunity arose once Ricky started writing songs. Dad had written songs for me before but somehow something didn't click. We tried with a few record companies a long time ago but I was desperate to go into it. I would have done anything in those days – I'd have sung any songs. I think I knew they weren't quite what I was into but I was going to take any kind of experience with open hands. And then Rick started writing songs, and 'cause he's a young writer and my brother, I related to what he was writing more than anyone else before. He asked me to demo 'Kids in America' after he'd written some other songs. I did it and we brought it to RAK and that's the story of my life.

Sally: And it happened straight away really.

Kim: Yes, it did. I mean, I'm a lucky cow, I really am. I know that.

Sally: Mickey Most is managing you now, isn't he?

Kim: He's been managing me up to now but management will become a separate thing in the future which my dad will take over. Mickey is the boss, but he always listens to me and Ricky and especially to Dad, and it's a very good working relationship. We don't feel stifled. We get on with the album and we do our own thing. I dress how I want to dress. I am how I want to be. I don't have someone hanging round me all the time saying, 'Don't say this – do say that'. It's really good.

Sally: It sounds a marvellous set up and obviously you're a very close family.

Kim: We are, but there's a lot of happy families in England. A lot of kids think it's hip not to have a happy family and that it's not hip to be happy. It's very unhip even to love your husband. It's ridiculous. I mean, I really can't believe in all that. People not wanting to love their husbands, people not wanting to love their families. It's rather like the generation gap, a stupid thing that's been accepted in our society. Our family's not pure bliss though. It's not 'The Waltons' by any stretch of imagination!

Sally: 'Kids in America' went to number two – a massive hit for a first record. Were you worried about how to follow it?

Kim: It didn't worry me the day I heard it had gone to number two. I just wallowed in my success for an hour, but I must admit I was a bit worried until we got 'Chequered Love'. Rick and Dad were writing a lot but we felt we didn't have the single. Then suddenly we got it, really quickly, and after that I was OK. For a while it didn't really hit me that I'd got to number two; it hit me in a bad way a lot later. I was getting very paranoid and I kept thinking something awful was going to happen because it had all been too good. We've got a great family and two babies which my mother desperately wanted, and I've got something I've always desperately wanted and everyone suddenly had got everything they wanted on a plate, and I thought, 'Something's got to give'. I got very paranoid about it for a week. And then I pulled myself out of it.

Sally: Will anything that you've written be on the album?

Kim: Yeah, I think it's going to be on the album, unless Dad comes up with something better and says, 'No, we can't have that'.

Sally: Do you think it's harder for women in this business? I was talking to Toyah about this the other day and she reckons that you have to be much harder as a woman to cope with it.

Kim: I don't know about Toyah because I don't know if she has, like I have, a father who's been in the business.

Sally: No, she hasn't. She's done it on her own.

Kim: Yes, exactly, so someone like Toyah would have to be harder, and most other girls, I think, have to be. Unfortunately, sometimes I think it shows; it's not too good. It's not their fault. It's just the way it is at the moment, but someone like me has a lot of worries taken care of.

Sally: You are shielded quite a bit, really, aren't you?

Kim: Yes, I am. If you have a family like I have it's OK when it's part of the business. It's hunky-dory, but there's a lot more to life than just getting on with business. There's the big matter of getting on with life, and life sometimes can get a bit tedious when you're growing up with a famous father and going to school. When you get success, you get a lot of, 'Oh, she did it on her dad's back', and all that sort of thing.

Sally: Did you get a lot of that?

Kim: Well, yes I did. I got a lot and Ricky got it, especially when he was being a pop star – that's why he stopped it, he couldn't handle it and, you know, people can really destroy you. I don't think they actually want to destroy you but they don't realise that by saying the things they do that they can almost put you off doing it for life.

Sally: There's been a lot written about your clothes, about the fact that you go to Oxfam and that you wear men's clothes. Do you still shop there?

Kim: I do, but I think there are better places to get clothes than Oxfam shops. Jumble sales are the best places to go. I do wear a lot of men's clothes, but I like wearing beautiful clothes as well. I bought a beautiful long black lace skirt the other day which I am going to make into a new romantic dress.

Sally: What music do you all listen to at home?

Kim: Well, my dad has this problem – as soon as the record player goes wrong, he goes out and buys a new one. It went wrong about six months ago and Dad still hasn't got round to going out and buying a new one. Probably the plug's fused or something, but he's just so lazy he can't get it together to fix it. I said to him, 'For God's sake, Dad, this is meant to be a musical family and we haven't got a record player except in my room'. He says, 'Yeah, I must go and buy a new one'. But I listen to a lot of music in my room. I like buying in Oxfam shops where you get albums you've never heard of. I buy all those up. But I like a lot of people. Elvis Costello is one of my favourites. I like a lot of the girl singers – the Motown ones and . . .

Sally: What about ambitions? Have you got it all mapped out or are you just happy with the way things are going at the moment?

Kim: I am quite happy with it. I don't really know what plans I have for next week, let alone beyond that.